BOOK ONE OF THE *BELIEVING AND*

Words lead to deeds...

REASON TO BELIEVE

they prepare the soul,

ANN WALSH

make it ready,

VERITAS

and move it to tenderness –

Teresa of Avila

First published 1994 by
Veritas Publications
7-8 Lower Abbey Street
Dublin 1

Imprimatur
✠ Desmond Connell
Archbishop of Dublin

ISBN 1 85390 277 2

The author gratefully acknowledges the work of
the Education Sub-Committee of the Episcopal
Commission on Catechetics, chaired by Bishop
Donal Murray, the contribution of the Post-
Primary Diocesan Advisors, and the participa-
tion of the teachers who piloted this text.

Design: Bill Bolger
Origination: The Type Bureau, Dublin
Printed in the Republic of Ireland by
Smurfit Web Press Ltd

Acknowledgements
The Thomas More Association, Chicago, Stories of
Faith, John Shea; St Mary's Press, Great Religions of of
the World, Loretta Pastva; The Furrow, article by
Gerald O'Collins, April 1990; Columba Press, Science
and the Bible, Sean Kealy; Brendan Kennelly, 'The
Good' and 'Moments when the Light'; Gill &
Macmillan, The Time of My Life, Gay Byrne, and Be
`Not Afraid, Jean Vanier; Paulist Press, What is
Religion? and What is God?, J.F. Haught; extracts from
Man's Search for Meaning, Victor Frankl, and
Blessings, Mary Craig, by permission of Hodder &
Stoughton Ltd; HarperCollins Publishers Ltd,
Gateway to God, Simone Weil, After Ideology, David
Walsh, Gulag Archipelago II, Aleksandr Solzhenitsyn,
and A New Path to the Waterfall, Raymond Carver;
The National Magazine Company Ltd, 'Me and God'
by Gillian Cooper, from Cosmopolitan Magazine, July
1993; John Murray (Publishers) Ltd, 'Christmas',
John Betjeman; The Tablet, article by Karl Rahner in
issue of 6 March 1971; Bantam Doubleday Dell
Publishing Group, Inc., Creative Ministry, Henri
Nouwen; Burns & Oates Ltd, Introduction to
Christian Faith and Jesus the Christ, Walter Kasper;
J.M. Dent & Sons Ltd, Publishers, 'The Kingdom',
R.S. Thomas; Padraig Daly OSA, 'Affair'; Word
Publishing, Understanding the New Age, Russell
Chandler; Twenty-Third Publications, P.O. Box 180,
Mystic, Connecticut 06355, Redemptive Intimacy; A

New Perspective for the Journey, copyright 1981 by
Dick Westley (paper, 176pp, US$5.95); Michael
Paul Gallagher SJ, Help My Unbelief (originally pub-
lished by Veritas Publications; now available from
Loyola University Press, Chicago); Darton,
Longman & Todd Ltd, Free to Believe, Michael Paul
Gallagher, God of Surprises, Gerard Hughes; Candle
in the Wind, Copyright 1960 by Aleksandr
Solzhenitsyn. Translation copyright 1973 by the
University of Minnesota. Published by the
University of Minnesota Press; New Dawn Music,
'Be Not Afraid; Bob Dufford; Faber & Faber Ltd,
Lord of the Flies, William Golding, 'The Love Song
of J. Alfred Prufrock' and Four Quartets, T.S. Eliot;
Routledge, Modern Man in Search of a Soul, Karl
Jung; Pan Books Ltd, The Diary of Anne Frank,
Penguin Books Ltd, Pensées, Blaise Pascal, A Rumour
of Angels, Peter Berger; The Irish Times, articles pub-
lished in December 1992 and September 1993;
Gallery Press and the estate of Patrick Kavanagh,
'The Great Hunger'; Henry Holt & Co. Inc. and the
estate of Robert Frost, 'The Road Not Taken';
Northern Songs Ltd, 'Nowhere Man', the Beatles,
and 'Imagine', John Lennon; excerpts from the
English translation of The Roman Missal © 1973,
Committee on English in the Liturgy, Inc. (ICEL).
All rights reserved. The Mystery of God, The Christian
Heritage and I Am With You Always are published by
Veritas Publications.

Illustrations
p.14 KNA Bild; pp. 9,16, National Gallery of
Ireland; pp.13, 32, 44, 77, 81, 85, 111, 115, 149,
169, Mary Evans Picture Library; p.18, The
National Magazine Company Ltd., p.53, Mary
Evans/Alexander Meledin Collection; pp. 15,73,
National Mission Council; pp. 19, 20, Bord Fáilte;
p.24, Radio Telefis Eireann; pp. 26, 109,179, 202,
Office of Public Works; pp. 29, 61, 174, Paul Peter
Piech; p. 48, Press Association; p.55, Luke
Golobitsh; p.59, Mary Ellen Mark; p.74, John
Sturruck/Network Photographers; pp.79, 125, 126,
130, 131, 138, 141, CIRIC; p.126, Philipe
Lissac/CIRIC; p. 91, NASA/Science Photo Library;
pp. 104, 135, 199, 206, Bill Doyle; pp. 108, 117,
Ancient Art and Architecture Collection; p. 148,
Museum of Antiquities, Newcastle-upon-Tyne; p.
153, The British Museum; p. 158, The Tate Gallery;
p. 187, The Imperial War Museum.

Contents

Section I

Chapter 1	The Situation of Faith	5
Chapter 2	Types of Unbelief	27
Chapter 3	Why do People Believe?	41
Chapter 4	'Modern Man in Search of a Soul'	65
Chapter 5	The Growth of Faith	88

Section II

Chapter 6	The Phenomenon of Religion	103
Chapter 7	Prehistoric Religion	113
Chapter 8	World Religions Today	120
Chapter 9	Judaism	137
Chapter 10	Christianity	144

Section III

Chapter 11	The Foundations of Christian Faith	155
Chapter 12	The Challenge of Christian Faith	168
Chapter 13	Evil and Suffering and the Challenge to Christian Faith	181
Chapter 14	'If Christ had not been raised from the dead your faith is in vain.'	195

The Second Vatican Council, called by Pope John XXIII, opened in October 1963 and lasted until 1965. It was a major event in the life of the Church – with the exception of Vatican I, which met in 1870, there had been no major council since the Council of Trent in the sixteenth century which considered the issues raised by the Reformation. Vatican II was concerned with faith and the Church in the modern world.

CHAPTER 1

The Situation of Faith

This chapter considers the question of faith today. It acknowledges that there has been a decline in faith in this part of the world and it traces some of the historical causes for this (Summary p.17). It examines why Ireland's experience and practice of faith has been unique.

Introduction

In 1965 the Second Vatican Council in its document *The Church in the Modern World* looked at the role of religious faith in the life of people of the twentieth century.

> As regards religion there is a completely new atmosphere...on the one hand people are taking a hard look at all magical world-views and prevailing superstitions and demand a more personal and active commitment of faith.... On the other hand greater numbers are falling away from the practice of religion. In the past it was the exception to (reject) God and religion to the point of abandoning them, and then only in individual cases; but nowadays it seems a matter of course to reject them as [out of tune] with scientific progress and a new kind of humanism.
> *Gaudium et spes*, 7

The situation of faith has changed dramatically in this century. While there are many who experience a more personal and adult faith, there are many more who abandon their faith. This is a completely new situation. In the words of T.S. Eliot:

> Men have left God not for other gods, they say, but for no god; and this has never happened before.

We can find evidence to support what is being said here if we analyse our own position on faith as we sit in a post-primary school in Ireland at the end of the twentieth century.

Thirty years ago it could well be assured that most pupils in a class believed in God and practised their faith. Individuals here or there might have doubted or rejected their faith but would usually have kept such attitudes to themselves. It can be difficult to be the odd one out. Moreover, the faith of the majority was backed up by the experience and practice of faith in the home, where weekly or even daily attendance at Mass was standard practice. In many instances the Rosary was said in the home while people often attended devotions or other religious services. The Sabbath and preparation for the Sabbath through confession on Saturday were big events in the week for many people. Religion played a major part in people's lives.

Pope John Paul II in Galway during his visit to Ireland in 1979

Young People and Faith Today

Consider how things have changed.

1. There are still many young people who believe in God and for whom faith is an important aspect of their lives. Indeed, there are some who say that this faith is even deeper than that of earlier generations, in so far as it is freely and personally chosen by young people themselves and is not a product of mere habit or mere conformity to the expectations of parents, parish or school. We often see this faith in practice when young people become involved in parish liturgies, in caring for the poor and the old and in their active awareness of world issues like civil rights, conservation and peace.

2. There are others for whom faith is a very private matter. They are reluctant to talk about it in a classroom situation, for example. Deep down they believe in God. They may pray alone and in private. Sometimes they may have difficulties with the Church. They may not see any connection between the God with whom they have a personal relationship and Church teaching and practice. Sometimes too they may not see any connection between their private faith and their daily interaction with other people and society as a whole.

3. There are still others for whom faith is becoming an increasingly irrelevant issue – a thing of their childhood past. Yes, they have been baptised, made their First Holy Communion and Confirmation, but religion no longer has meaning for them. It is not so much that they have made a deliberate decision to abandon their faith. Rather what they see as religious issues no longer hold any interest for them. They have enough meaning in their lives to keep them going without needing to turn to religion. They do not reject God in a very deliberate manner. They simply drift out of faith almost unconsciously. They have plenty of other distractions.

4. Then there are those who live very good and moral lives. They are concerned about the world and their fellow human beings. They would like to devote their lives to improving the lot of humankind. They are what might be called good humanists. (A humanist is someone who is concerned about the welfare of human beings.) However, they do not see faith as necessary to what they do. They want to help their fellow human beings because they value people and are concerned for the quality of human life. They do not see the need to bring God into it. Indeed some of them would argue that religion would take from what they do. They want to be seen to be helping people for their own sake and not because they might be rewarded for doing so in an afterlife.

5. Finally, there are those who reject God and religion out of hand. They see religion as a thing of the past or something associated with other cultures which are not seen to be as 'advanced' as the western world. They see God as unnecessary in a modern, technological

world. Some of the more hostile would see religion as limiting human freedom or causing needless guilt. Others simply say it belongs to another age: we have progressed beyond it!

Questions
1. Do you fit into any of the categories described here? Explain.
2. Who/what has influenced your attitude to faith? How have you been influenced?

Why has the Situation of Faith Changed?

As we examine our own position on faith, we may find that we fit into one or other of the categories above, or we may find that our attitude to faith is not quite like that of any of the people described. One way or another, it may well be a new experience for us to consider our faith at all. It may be an even newer experience for us to ask ourselves why we hold the positions we do.

There are many personal reasons why we believe or do not believe. Equally, because we are part of society and of history, there are both external and historical factors that help us explain why we think and act as we do about religion today.

People look at history not just to find out about the past but also to understand the present. A knowledge of the events of history helps to explain why we are the way we are today. Religion and Church are part of the history of humankind and so the changes that have taken place in history affect the story of faith. That is why we now consider some of the historical movements which have affected Christian faith in the western world.

Question
Can you think of anything that we think or do today that has been influenced by our history?

Historical Movements and their Effects on Faith

1. THE ENLIGHTENMENT – THE AGE OF REASON

For many historians the modern world begins with the Enlightenment, and so this is our starting-point for looking at the roots of the situation of faith that we now experience in the twentieth century.

The Enlightenment was an intellectual movement that examined the whole of eighteenth-century civilisation, e.g. law, politics, religion, education, economics etc., pointing out its weaknesses and suggesting ways of improvement.

There were two main features of the Enlightenment or 'Age of Reason', as it was called.

Sir Robert Waller and his son Robert, by Robert Hunter. *Courtesy of The National Gallery of Ireland.*

 Questions
1. How do you respond to this painting?
2. Has your use of reason influenced your response?

a. The Emphasis on Reason

During this 'Age of Reason', people questioned everything. They were looking for reasonable, scientific explanations for things that happened and for the way things were. They were no longer satisfied, as people in the Middle Ages were, with the idea that something was 'the will of God' and so beyond human understanding. They wanted to rely on reason and knowledge instead of faith and trust.

Isaac Newton, 1642-1727

Scientists began carrying out experiments and so came up with explanations that they could prove – Isaac Newton's Law of Gravity explained how the sun and planets stayed in place. As a result of such discoveries people in the eighteenth century began to feel that they were wiser or more 'enlightened' than the people who had gone before them. They stopped believing in magic and in witchcraft and some stopped believing in God. If God could not be fully explained by human reason alone, then his existence could be called into question. As one English philosopher, John Locke, put it, 'Reason must be our last judge and guide in everything'.

Questions
1. Do you agree totally with Locke?
2. What aspects of human nature does Locke neglect?

b. The Challenge to Authority

Other aspects of the Enlightenment also affected faith. Philosophers like Locke, Voltaire and Rousseau questioned how people were ruled. Rousseau summed up the attitude of these philosophers when he wrote 'Man is born free but is everywhere in chains'. He went on to demand the right to liberty, property and equality for all. He called for the 'sovereignty of the people', where the people are the source of all State power. Rulers merely represent the wishes of the people.

Such thinking was to help bring about the French Revolution, the collapse of the monarchy and the Declaration of the Rights of Man. The authority of the King had not just been questioned – it was replaced by the authority of the people. It was only a matter of time until all sources of authority, including the Church, were challenged. People wanted freedom from authority, whether of the State or the Church. They wanted to be free to think and act for themselves. They did not want to be told what to do.

Question
Why do some people not like certain systems and structures?

2. THE INDUSTRIAL REVOLUTION AND THE RISE OF SOCIALISM

The Industrial Revolution which began in Britain in the mid-eighteenth century was to cause many changes in people's lives. While the early years of the Industrial Revolution brought mostly misery to workers, in time, mass production meant that people could buy goods cheaply and easily. Better and cheaper travel facilities meant that whereas in the past most people never travelled very far from their place of birth, now they could travel to cities and even to other countries where they would be exposed to new ideas and experiences. This was to have two effects on religion.

Casting a cylinder for a steamship at a Millwall iron foundry in 1854

a. Religion was replaced as a source of meaning

Work, pay, holidays and material goods were now becoming very important to people, sometimes replacing religion as a source of meaning in their lives. As people became better off, they had more to occupy and interest them and so religion often moved to the periphery of their lives. Contrast this with the Middle Ages when religion was part of every aspect of life – work, leisure, education, art, music. Now often the only specifically religious act of many people became attendance at Mass on Sunday morning. Religion and life were being divorced from one another.

b. Human rather than divine solutions to world problems

Karl Marx

The other side of the Industrial Revolution was the oppression and exploitation of workers. At a time when the wealth generated by mass production benefited only the wealthy factory owners, and trade unions were banned, life was very difficult for the average worker. It was such misery and his own experience of poverty while living in London that influenced the German thinker, Karl Marx (1818-83), the founder of Communism. When he looked at the lives of workers he said that it was religion that was preventing them from improving their situation. How was this so? According to Marx, religion was the 'opium of the people'. Like any other drug it helped people to forget about their misery but it did nothing to solve their problems. Religion promised them another world – heaven – where they will be rewarded for putting up with this one. They are so caught up with this other world that they do nothing to improve their lot in this world. Marx wanted to get rid of religion and make people see that they could solve their own problems here and now. They should overthrow the capitalist system and bring about a new world where the good things of life would be shared out equally between everyone. This would be heaven on earth and so people would no longer need religion and its promise of a reward in heaven. It would be human happiness brought about by human effort.

The most significant attempt to put Marx's theories into practice was made in Russia in 1917, when the first Communist state was set up. Atheism became official policy in Russia and other communist states, though it can be argued that it was held in place more by force than by the will of the people.

Question
Is it true to say that human happiness depends on human effort?

3. THE SCIENTIFIC AND TECHNOLOGICAL REVOLUTIONS

The scientific and technological revolutions were to have three main effects on religious faith.

a. Scientific truth becomes the only truth

When discussing the Enlightenment we referred briefly to the effect that the scientific 'proof mentality' had on faith. This effect becomes more obvious in the nineteenth century which was not just a time of great human inventiveness (Industrial and Agricultural Revolutions), but also of great advances in the field of science. This was a time when spectacular discoveries helped people to understand better how the world around them worked. It was an age of

Charles Darwin

13

experiment when scientists studied the problems of nature more closely and experiments often yielded amazing results – results that could be demonstrated and scientifically proven. What effect was this to have on religious faith? The scientific revolution gave rise to what could be called the 'proof mentality'. This meant that beliefs or viewpoints that could not be subjected to or proven by scientific analysis were suspected or discarded completely. Scientific truth became the only form of truth. So if God and his existence could not be proven scientifically, it was doubted or denied.

b. Science and religion clash

Galileo

In some instances, scientists and Churchmen clashed with one another. In the seventeenth century Galileo Galilei (1564-1642) was condemned by the Holy Office in Rome when, as a result of the invention of the telescope, he concluded that the earth moved around the sun, not the sun around the earth, as the Bible said. In the nineteenth century when the biologist Charles Darwin (1809-82) put forward the theory of evolution, he was condemned because his thinking seemed to conflict with the biblical account of Creation. The result of such condemnation was that religion was discredited in the minds of many who considered themselves enlightened by scientific thinking. At its worst, this clash led to the conclusion that the truth of science was the only truth and that religious thinking was backward and immature.

c. The emphasis on human ability and the visible world

The scientific revolution emphasised the human being and human abilities. Science and technology enable human beings to make themselves increasingly 'lords and masters' of the real world, able to plan and control it. No longer do they need to look to God. The result is, as the German theologian, Bishop Walter Kasper, puts it, a 'world in which we encounter less and less often the traces of God and more and more often the marks of man'. Furthermore the emphasis on 'this world' and the 'real world' has given rise to what is called 'secularism', derived from the Latin *saeculum* (which means 'world'). Secularism is the belief that 'this world', the immediate environment that is visible and open to scientific investigation, is all there is to reality. Therefore any idea of God, of another world, of an 'ultimate' reality, is rejected. Thus we become the 'measure of all things' and this world becomes our 'paradise'.

Questions and exercises
1. List the things that are important to you.
2. Examine the sources of happiness in your life. How secular, how caught up in the things of this world are you?
3. Note any elements in your answer which suggest or point to something beyond this world.

4. EDUCATION, THE REVOLUTION IN COMMUNICATIONS AND THE PLURALIST SOCIETY

Pluralism can be understood as an attitude of mind that accepts more than one way of thinking, acting or being. It is the opposite of monism where only one way is acceptable, or simply prevails. A pluralist society is one in which different groups preserve their own customs and beliefs and so many views and value-systems exist together, sometimes peacefully, sometimes not. The USA is probably the best example of such a society where people of different race, colour and creed live and work side by side. Libya is an example of a monist society where even visitors have to conform to religious and civil law.

In the past, monism was the norm. In the Middle Ages, for example, religion permeated every aspect of human life. This was possible because people were only exposed to the influences of one locality, of one Church, of one society, where attitudes and value systems were

Village life in Nigeria

15

fairly similar. They rarely knew how people outside of their culture lived or how they thought or what they believed. For most there was only one way of being – theirs.

Mass communication and the widespread availability of education have changed all of this. Now people have increased knowledge of different ways of life and of different value systems. They realise that their set of beliefs and practices is not the only one.

Still Life
by Juan Gris.
*Courtesy of The
National Gallery
of Ireland.*

Questions
1. What do you find unusual about this picture?
2. How do you think your grandparents would have reacted to this picture?
3. Why might there be a difference between your reaction to the picture and theirs?

EFFECTS ON RELIGION

In such a society, religious faith is seen as just one option amongst the many influences. Often the other options seem more progressive and so more attractive. This is partly because a pluralist society promotes a liberal frame of mind which is seen to be open to change. Ideas, structures and organisations which are deemed conservative (opposed to change) do not get much support.

A Church that is perceived to be conservative, particularly on moral issues like contraception and divorce, does not get much support in a society where people are presented with a variety of options and want to be free to decide on such issues for themselves. People are not attracted to organisations or beliefs that seem to limit their freedom.

Summary of Historical Movements and their Influence on Religious Faith

Historical Movement	Features	Effect on Religious Faith
THE ENLIGHTENMENT	1. Emphasised reason 2. Challenged authority	1. If God could not be understood by human reason alone his existence was doubted. 2. The authority of the Church was challenged.
THE INDUSTRIAL REVOLUTION AND THE RISE OF SOCIALISM	1. Rise in material wealth for some 2. Exploitation of workers	1. Material wealth made God seem superfluous in people's lives. 2. Karl Marx called on people to abandon the opium of religion and solve their own problems.
THE SCIENTIFIC REVOLUTION	1. Scientific proof/truth became the only form of proof/truth. 2. Human beings were seen as Masters of the Universe. 3. This world became the only world.	1. Religious faith/truth was suspected. 2. The human being replaced God as all-powerful. 3. The idea of the 'other world' was abandoned.
EDUCATION AND MASS COMMUNICATION	1. Led to the pluralist society 2. Led to the rise of liberalism – desire for human freedom	1. Religious faith became just one amongst many options. 2. The Church was seen as conservative and therefore a limit on freedom.

The twentieth century witnessed a decline in Christian faith in the western world. In summary we can say that this was because of the absolute belief that human beings, through the wonders of science, industrialisation and education, were capable of providing for human happiness. As we approach the twenty-first century, whether it is because of the collapse of communism, the inability of so many governments to tackle unemployment, the wars that still wage or the millions who still die in our world from starvation, people are beginning to wonder whether, indeed, human beings have all the answers. The scientific and technological revolutions which emphasised human ability and promised so much do not seem to have delivered on such promises – at least not for all. Indeed, one writer goes so far as to say:

> The age that began with the glory of the Renaissance, the bright expectations of the Enlightenment, and the energies of the scientific, industrial and political revolutions has devolved into the horror of the twentieth century. (*After Ideology*, D. Walsh)

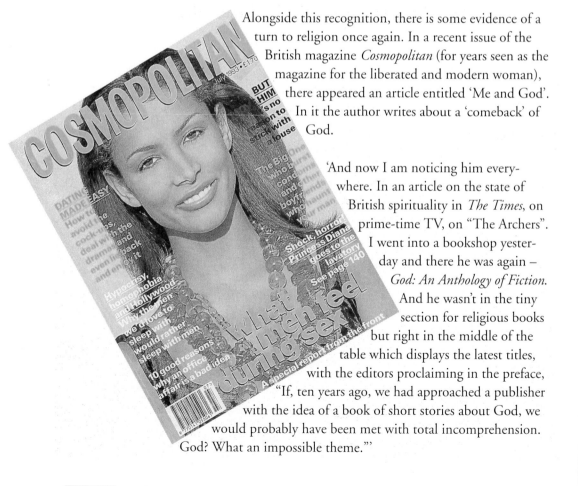

Alongside this recognition, there is some evidence of a turn to religion once again. In a recent issue of the British magazine *Cosmopolitan* (for years seen as the magazine for the liberated and modern woman), there appeared an article entitled 'Me and God'. In it the author writes about a 'comeback' of God.

'And now I am noticing him every-where. In an article on the state of British spirituality in *The Times*, on prime-time TV, on "The Archers". I went into a bookshop yester-day and there he was again – *God: An Anthology of Fiction*. And he wasn't in the tiny section for religious books but right in the middle of the table which displays the latest titles, with the editors proclaiming in the preface, "If, ten years ago, we had approached a publisher with the idea of a book of short stories about God, we would probably have been met with total incomprehension. God? What an impossible theme."'

The writer goes on to give her reasons for the return to the idea of God:

> We have been shattered by the fall of communism and the demise of socialism. We are feeling insecure because of the recession. We're rejecting the materialism of the eighties. We have discovered – and it has only taken 30 years – that sex and romance are not the answer to our deepest problems...... However politically incorrect it may be, human beings have an intrinsic need for faith. (*Cosmopolitan*, July 1993)

Question
Do you agree that there has been a return to God? Give reasons for your answer.

THE SITUATION OF FAITH IN IRELAND

For a long time, Ireland escaped many of the influences that led to the decline in faith experienced in most European countries. This can be partly explained by

a. the characteristics of Irish Christianity
b. the association of Catholicism and nationalism

The characteristics of Irish Christianity

A NATURAL RELIGIOUS SENSE

If we go right back before the time of St Patrick, we find in the Celts a natural religious spirit. In their art, their mythology and their druids, we find an openness to what we might

later label religious mystery – an awareness of something greater and beyond this world. We know, for instance, that they believed in the immortality of the soul and paid religious honour to the forces of nature.

When St Patrick came to Ireland, he came among a people who were already religious by nature. While there was opposition to this new religion of Christianity it is interesting to note that Ireland was unique among all the countries of western Europe in so far as her conversion produced no martyrs. Thus the elements of Christianity cannot be so alien to these people. Indeed, in 'converting' the people, it can be argued that St Patrick was building upon their traditional religious devotion.

As Christianity developed in Ireland, this native, natural religious sense was to remain its dominant feature. While Europe focused on the Roman model of basilicas, processions and ceremonies, in Ireland, until the nineteenth century, the faith and religious practices of the people, rather than the influence of the organised Church, were to be the hallmark of Catholicism. We see this early on with the development of the monasteries, where religious communities of men and women were the most important centres of religion in Ireland. As the late Cardinal Tomás Ó Fiaich noted, Ireland was unusual in that its most important churches were ruled by abbots, many of whom were not bishops, and eventually the monastic system replaced dioceses altogether.

In his study of the history of Irish Catholicism, John J. Ó Ríordáin CSSR identified the following elements:

GOD AS CLOSE TO ONE'S LIFE

Thus the Irish Church was very locally based and community-minded. This meant that religion was something near to people. We see an example of this in one of the names they had for God – 'Rí' (King). However this was not a king in the European experience of monarchy – someone remote and unknown. The 'Rí' ruled the 'tuaith', of which there were over 150 in the country. So the king could be the neighbour's son. God was perceived as being very near, as we see in St Patrick's 'Breastplate':

> Christ be with me, Christ within me,
> Christ behind me, Christ before me,
> Christ beside me, Christ to win me,
> Christ to comfort and restore me,
> Christ beneath me, Christ above me,
> Christ in quiet, Christ in danger,
> Christ in hearts of all that love me,
> Christ in mouth of friend and stranger.

God's presence in creation is another marked feature of Celtic Christianity, as we see in this ancient poem describing heaven.

GOD'S PRESENCE IN NATURE

> Round the tree of life the flowers
> are ranged, abundant, even;
> its crest on every side spreads out
> on the fields and plains of heaven.
>
> Glorious flocks of singing birds
> celebrate their truth,
> green abounding branches bear
> choicest leaves and fruit.
>
> The lovely flocks maintain their song
> in the changeless weather,
> A hundred feathers for every bird,
> A hundred tunes for every feather.

Questions
1. What image of God is presented in this poem?
2. Do you find this image of God attractive?

THE LOVE OF GOD AND THE LOVE OF ONE'S NEIGHBOUR

The link between love of God and love of one's neighbour is yet another feature of Irish Christianity.

> God in Heaven!
> The door of my house will always be
> open to every traveller
> May Christ open his to me!
>
> If you have a guest
> and deny him anything in the house,
> it's not the guest you hurt.
> It's Christ you refuse.

Even in prayer, as Fr John J. Ó Ríordáin notes, any form of lack of hospitality, of lack of concern for one's neighbour is frowned upon.

> A prayer made for oneself alone is known in Irish as a 'paidir gann', literally a 'scarce prayer', or a 'stingy prayer' (*Irish Catholics*).

Pilgrimage was to be another feature of Irish Christianity which continues to this very day. Early pilgrims chose places like Rome, Jerusalem or Santiago di Compostella in Spain. At home, places like Clonmacnois, Glendalough, Croagh Patrick and St Patrick's Purgatory were to be popular places for prayer and repentance. Many of these are still places of pilgrimage for people today.

The Irish-Gaelic experience of Christianity involves:

> – a natural religious sense
> – an experience of God as close to one's life
> – an awareness of his presence in nature
> – a link between the love of God and love of one's neighbour
> – the importance of pilgrimage

Some features of this experience still survive. They contribute to making us the kind of people we are. As the French scholar Coquebert noted on his visit to Kerry and the south-west in 1790:

> The goodness of these people reveals itself in their love of children and in their kindness to strangers. When they give charity they do so with an air of politeness to avoid humiliating the recipient and the best place at the fire is reserved for the poor man.

Even as people become disenchanted with organised religion our unique Christian heritage may well be why the words of the poet Patrick Kavanagh still ring true, in this description of a farmer ploughing:

> No worry on Maguire's mind this day
> Except that he forgot to bring his matches.
> 'Hop back there Polly, hoy back, woa, wae,'
> From every second hill a neighbour watches
> With all the sharpened interest of rivalry.
>
> Yet sometimes when the sun comes through a gap
> These men know God the Father in a tree:
> The Holy Spirit is the rising sap,
> and Christ will be the green leaves that will come
> at Easter from the sealed and guarded tomb.
>
> 'The Great Hunger'

Pilgrims climbing Croagh Patrick

Question
1. Do you think the traditional Irish-Gaelic experience of Christianity is part of our religious sense today? Explain.

Catholicism and Nationalism

Through the nineteenth century and into the twentieth century, to be Irish was to be Catholic, to strive for an independent Ireland, free from Protestant British rule. Movements like Daniel O'Connell's campaigns for Catholic Emancipation and Repeal in the 1820s and 1840s are probably the best examples of the Church and its link with constitutional nationalism in the nineteenth century.

RTE's first television broadcast from O'Connell Street, Dublin, New Year's Eve 1961

Irish independence was won in 1921 and the next forty years or so would be spent trying to establish the new State and its people as different from and independent of Britain, able to take her own distinct place among the nations of the world. This Ireland would be unique. In the words of Eamon de Valera, it would be 'a land whose countryside would be bright with cosy homesteads, whose fields and villages would be joyous with the sounds of industry, with the rompings of sturdy children, the contests of athletic youths and the laughter of comely maidens, whose firesides would be forums for the wisdom of serene old age'.

As a result there was a suspicion of and lack of welcome for foreign influences. Furthermore, Ireland did not experience an industrial revolution in the first half of this century and, in the absence of free education, television and foreign travel, not many were exposed to scientific thinking or to the hallmarks of a pluralism being experienced elsewhere in the western world.

The 1960s were to change all of this. In 1959 Eamon de Valera resigned as Taoiseach and was replaced by Sean Lemass, who was to undertake a programme for economic development. Economics, not nationalism, was becoming the dominant value in Irish politics. Ireland was becoming more prosperous. New jobs were created, emigrants returned home and the standard of living rose. Foreign holidays began to be more and more common. In 1961 Telefís Eireann, Ireland's first television station, began broadcasting. In 1966, Donough O'Malley introduced free secondary education for all. By the time Ireland became a member of the European Economic Community in 1973, we were no longer seen as an isolated island on the periphery of Europe. We were now being exposed to the culture, beliefs and value systems of the rest of the world. We were becoming a different kind of society – more urban, better educated and widely travelled. Such social changes were to affect religious faith and practice, as seen in this chart:

KIND OF SOCIETY	POSITION OF THE CHURCH	TYPE OF UNBELIEF FOUND
1. Stable, rural	1. Dominant, central	1. Non-practice by isolated individuals
2. Less rural and wealthier	2. Religion an increasingly separate sphere; one influence among others	2. Sub-groups (youth, workers etc.) fall away
3. Urban, technological, complex	3. A marginal institution (including non-practice)	3. Non-belief by masses

Help my Unbelief, Michael Paul Gallagher

The position of the Church is still more dominant in Ireland than in other countries. As Bishop Donal Murray notes in *The Future of the Faith:*

> The truth is that the influence of the Church in social life and in public policy is both less than it *was* in Ireland and greater than it *is* in most other countries.

While there is still a very high level of practice in this country (see surveys), there is growing evidence that alongside such high church attendance there are some for whom the teaching of the Church, particularly on moral issues such as divorce and contraception, is seen as either irrelevant or an intrusion. The result is that, for many, religion is pushed into a corner where it is allowed to have little or no influence on people's attitudes or way of living. This means that while open hostility and rejection of God is not so common, indifference towards the Church and its teaching is increasing.

Revision questions and exercises

1. Describe the situation of faith today.
2. Why has the situation of faith changed?
3. Why has Ireland's experience of Christianity been unique?
4. Write an essay on the future of faith.
5. Examine your personal faith since childhood with some of the following things in mind:
   – how your faith has changed;
   – the influences on your own religious development;
   – the importance or otherwise of faith in your life at present.

The loaves and fishes. Detail from Moone high cross.

CHAPTER 2

Types of Unbelief

This chapter outlines five possible types of unbelief:

1. What is termed 'Church' atheism, where people have problems with the Church rather than with God as such.
2. Intellectual atheism – a thought-out rejection of God.
3. Psychological atheism – where someone rejects God because of certain negative experiences he/she has had.
4. Secular atheism – where God is pushed aside because of the attractions of the world.
5. Where God is rejected because of the image, often the false image that people have of God.

Introduction

To study the question of 'unbelief' in Ireland is a complex task. On the one hand, Ireland has the image of being a very Catholic country. Such an image is created by the fact that by comparison with any other country in the western world, Ireland has a high level of Church practice, particularly Mass attendance. A 1973 survey showed that 91% of Catholics attended Mass regularly. By 1981 this had fallen to 80% and the most recent survey shows that 80% still attend Mass on a regular basis. Church practice remains very high in this country, particularly when one compares it with Quebec, a French-speaking province in Canada where, in the 1960s alone, Mass attendance fell from 65% to about 30%. In France between 1971 and 1975 there was a drop of 40% in Mass attendance. At other levels too, Ireland is seen to be more influenced by Catholic or religious values than most other countries. For instance, we are now the only country in the EC that has legislation banning abortion and divorce. Many schools and hospitals are managed by religious. While there is some increase in registry office marriages, they are very few in number by comparison with Church marriages.

However, this is not the full story. Take, for instance, attendance at sacraments, which for the most part still remains very high. In many cases, it is easier to 'opt into' sacraments like Baptism, Holy Communion, Confirmation and Marriage, than it is to 'opt out' of them. As a result of social and family pressures, many people partake of these sacraments and allow their children to do so because it seems the easy way out. To opt out might cause family conflict and division.

We see such a scenario in the closing pages of John Broderick's novel, *An Apology for Roses*, which analyses the attitudes of a growing middle class in a midlands town. A young couple are planning their wedding. 'Religion' seems irrelevant to them but they have to go through with the formula of a Church marriage to please the family. Are they going to receive Communion? That would mean Confession which would make each of them feel 'an awful hypocrite'. They decide to say nothing in advance but simply not go to Communion. And this conversation ends ironically with Marie warning Brian that he will have to conform and start going to Mass again after marriage. 'It isn't so bad once you get into the habit which is all it is really. I don't think there is any point in making an issue of it. After all, neither of us cares that much any more. I wonder if anybody really does. And you meet people, keep up with the news and that sort of thing. Although of course the sermons are diabolical.'

Questions
1. Is Mass attendance simply a habit?
2. Are habits necessarily bad?
3. What should go along with rituals or habits to make them authentic or meaningful?

So the high level of the practice of such sacraments can be deceptive. It does not, as we can see from Marie's comments, necessarily imply a deep level of faith or conviction. This becomes more obvious when one considers the one sacrament that is not so public and demands a more personal decision – namely the Sacrament of Reconciliation. Attendance at this sacrament has fallen more than at any other sacrament. Is this because, more than the other sacraments, the Sacrament of Reconciliation demands some personal examination of one's life, some sense of sin, some sense of belief in a loving God, and if these things don't exist, the sacrament makes no sense? So the story of unbelief in Ireland is complex and is influenced by many factors.

Questions
1. How do you think you would have reacted if your parents had told you that you could not make your First Communion or Confirmation until you were an adult?
2. If you do not believe or practise your faith at present, do you see yourself marrying in a Catholic church and baptising your children in the future?

I like your Christ,

I do not like your Christians.

Your Christians are so unlike your Christ.

Mahatma Gandhi

Church 'Atheism'

With the story of Marie and Brian we saw a situation where there was Church practice but without too much faith. The other side of this coin is a sense of disappointment, anger or indifference towards the Church. The sense of disappointment can be seen in the story of David, a bank official in his mid-twenties. 'Yes, I continue to go to Mass pretty regularly – but why I don't know. It's not simply to please the parents because I often go even when away from home. It's out of some sense of God but, like my hair, that sense of God is receding slowly. I hardly ever go to Communion, and I seldom feel in touch with God through Mass. My impression is that most of my friends, even if they practise, are completely untouched by it. It's something vaguely 'good' or safe that we keep doing because it seems better to go than not to go. Faith isn't dead for me, but it's not too alive either, and I suppose I come away most Sundays a bit disappointed, as if I was looking for something that I never get. There are times when I doubt the whole thing, but for some reason I still hang in there.' (*Help My Unbelief*, Michael Paul Gallagher)

Many people find themselves in David's shoes – having been brought up in the Catholic Church they still 'hang in there' out of some sense of loyalty or feeling good, but yet find themselves bored and frustrated with what they see as the Church's lack of challenge or relevance to their concerns. As Bishop Donal Murray puts it, 'many young people appear to see religion and the Church as having little relevance to some of their major concerns: the nuclear and environmental threats, the search for justice, the challenge of living humanly in a world of high unemployment and serious inequalities'. Sometimes such people leave the Church and join new cults or religious sects that appeal to them because they seem more inspiring, more demanding than the Church they were brought up in. They feel more personally involved and challenged than they did in the Church of their parents.

At another level, many young people see the Church as interfering with and limiting their freedom, particularly in sexual matters. The image of the Church as negative and closed can be summed up in the words of Brian Moore, who, looking back on his Catholic upbringing in Belfast, wrote, 'In the beginning was the word, and the word was No'.

There are many, too, who accuse the Church and believers of not living up to the ideal presented to them by Christ .

> I like your Christ,
> I do not like your Christians.
> Your Christians are so unlike your Christ.
> (Mahatma Gandhi)

The Second Vatican Council acknowledged this when it said that 'believers can have more than a little to do with the rise of atheism'. In this case when people reject the Church, they reject God too. The Irish Bishops, in their Lenten Pastoral of 1980, admitted this also.

> The biggest obstacle to Christian faith today is not intellectual doubt. It is, quite simply, the unChristian life-style of so many of us who think we are good Christians.
>
> *Handing on the Faith in the Home*

We remember, too, the philosopher Nietzsche's criticism of Christ and Christians – 'His followers should look more redeemed'.

Questions
1. Do you agree with Gandhi? Why/Why not?
2. How do you think Christians could be more like Christ?
3. Are there ways in which you think you might be hypocritical about your own faith?
4. Should the Church challenge Christians more? How?

Intellectual Atheism

a. Ludwig Feuerbach

On the west side of the city of Nuremberg, along the River Pegnity, the German philosopher Ludwig Feuerbach is buried. The grey stone covering his grave has his profile in bronze and the words 'born 1804, died 1874'. It was Feuerbach who first concluded that the Christian God was nothing more than the product of wishful thinking and that religion prevented us from recognising our own real worth and working to improve our life and our world. It was such thinking that was to influence a fellow German, Karl Marx.

b. Albert Camus

In his book *The Stranger,* the French philosopher Albert Camus tells this story.

> A Chaplain speaks to a condemned murderer: 'Why....don't you let me come to see you?' I explained that I didn't believe in God. 'Are you really so sure of that'?
> I said that I saw no point in troubling my head about the matter....
> 'God can help you. All the men I have seen in your position turned to Him in their time of trouble'.
> Obviously, I replied, they were at liberty to do so, if they felt like it. I, however, didn't want to be helped, and I hadn't time to work up interest for something that didn't interest me.

Question
What does the prisoner's response to the chaplain tell us about his attitude to faith?

Friedrich Nietzsche.

Camus believed that Christianity had died in Europe. Although he regarded this as a tragedy, he believed that there was nothing to be gained by harking back to the comforts and reassurances of Christianity, even in the face of death. Whatever meaning or comfort can be found in the world must come from a human rather than a divine source.

Nietzsche was born near Leipzig in Germany in 1844. His central idea as a philosopher was that Germany, like the rest of Europe, had turned against Christianity but refused to face up to this fact. A new culture had replaced the traditional religious culture – science had replaced religion. Since God does not exist, we must force meaning on our own lives.

c. Friedrich Nietzsche

The nineteenth-century philosopher Friedrich Nietzsche (1844-1900) is best known for his statement 'God is Dead'. Nietzsche looked around at his fellow human beings and discovered that to all intents and purposes, the idea of God had little meaning for him.

> Where has God gone? I shall tell you God is dead. What are these Churches now if they are not the tombs of God?

God had already died in the world and in people's hearts but, according to Nietzsche, they had failed to realise the consequences of the death of God.

> What did we do when we unchained this earth from its sun? Whither is it now moving? Away from all suns? Are we not ever rushing onwards, sidewards, forwards, to all sides? Is there still an above and a below? Are we not wandering in a never-ending nothingness?

Question

1. What does Nietzsche mean by his statement on the consequences of the death of God?
2. Do you agree with Nietzsche that without belief in God, we are 'wandering in an never-ending nothingness'?

What gives meaning to our life and death if God does not exist? We cannot fall back on the comfort of believing in God. We must create our own meaning.

What we find here in the writings of Feuerbach, Camus and Nietzsche is a more thought-out rejection of God. Such intellectual atheism is often the product of philosophical or scientific thinking. *Philosophy* can be defined as the search for wisdom and knowledge. This includes a search for the meaning and purpose of life. The big questions of philosophy are *Identity* (Who am I?), *Truth* (What can I know?), *Morality* (What must I do?), and *Ultimate meaning* (What can I hope for – beyond this world?). In so far as religion is supposed to give meaning to life, the philosopher considers the question of God. Some philosophers conclude that God is the ultimate source of meaning in life while others, like Feuerbach, Camus and Nietzsche, conclude that God is either dead or never existed, and so life is either absurd and meaningless (Camus) or we create our own meaning for living (Feuerbach, Nietzsche).

The other argument that rejects the existence of God arises out of *scientific thinking*. Such an argument concludes that the teachings of modern science replace what was called 'God of the gaps', whereby God was used to explain those things for which we had no other explanation. This is the kind of view put forward by Hubert, a student welfare officer.

> Certainly, for me, there's no rational – there's no reasonable argument to put up for God existing....To me, my world is explained, my daily life is explained by the fact that we know where we came from – we know how we arrived, where we are biologically, and we have history to tell us. There's no room in that for me, for some sort of mystical view of there being somebody or something around the place or up there or wherever, directing all of this, starting it all up and making sure that we keep on the same road. Is God necessary? To me it is just a totally unnecessary idea. We don't need God to explain why we are here. We don't need God to explain why the trees grow, why the world revolves on its axis, why it spins around the sun – which were supposedly, the proofs of God in the Middle Ages.

Question
How would an atheist defend her or his position?

Psychological Atheism

A third and perhaps more deeply personal form of atheism is psychological atheism, or what Michael Paul Gallagher terms 'atheism by reaction'. In this case, a person finds faith impossible because of an unhappy life or some negative experience. The idea of a God of love is sometimes just too incredible for someone who has never experienced love. The idea of faith is just too difficult for someone who finds trust difficult because they have been badly let down. An extreme account of such a situation is found in Jean Vanier's book *Be not Afraid.*

There was a girl in one of the large asylums in Paris, strapped to her bed, because otherwise she would scratch her face and eyes. The doctor said it was partly his fault that she was like this. Three years ago, she came to the hospital; she had to be spoon-fed, she did not move her eyes, she did not react to words. The only thing she reacted to was food – if she liked it she would smile, if not she would vomit. The doctor decided to reach her. He spent a lot of time with the girl. He fed her, he touched her, linking her relationship with food to a person, himself. This is the way children begin life, by food and touch in the arms of the mother, gradually moving on to other relatives, like a toy or other people. So this girl, at the age of fourteen or so, opened to reality, but reality for a girl like this is not a toy or the table or the bed, but a person. And so the doctor became everything to her, became her all.

And then he stopped seeing her. He had completed his experiment. From that moment she tried to commit suicide in a violent way. She had probably been deeply hurt when she was a tiny child, and she had closed herself off from reality, which was hell. For the weakness of a child demands a relationship with a person who can understand his delicacy and weakness. If he is treated with harshness and rejection, he will close himself off from a world that hates him. This is what the girl did until the doctor drew her forth and she came to trust him. And then she was dropped. She knew she was not wanted. So she went into a more violent form of suicide and she will stay that way, with her hands bandaged to her bed. She will certainly not succumb to the temptation of meeting someone again.

Question
1. Do you think our experience of life affects our view of God? Explain.

A less dramatic story is told by Michael Paul Gallagher in *Help my Unbelief.*

One day a student was discussing his essay with me when, out of the blue, he announced in a pretty aggressive manner, 'I'm an atheist, you know....' He came back a few days later, saying that he wanted to talk things over. His tone was a bit tense, but his very coming back said a lot. He started by announcing that there was something difficult he had to tell me about himself. He beat around the bush a little, then said, 'I suffer from asthma'.... Asthma had ruined his childhood, had cut him off from a lot of life, and became something he was ashamed of, and deeply angry over... That day I had an important insight, and I now assume that behind many an aggressive rejection ('I'm an atheist') there can live a softer reality of disappointment or hurt ('I suffer from asthma').

So one's experience of life can have much more to do with one's unbelief than any thought-out arguments about the existence of God. As Karl Rahner, the German theologian, put it:

The real argument against Christianity is this experience of darkness. I have always found that behind the technical arguments levelled against Christianity... there are always various experiences of life causing the spirit and the heart to be dark, tired and despairing.

The 'technical arguments' that Rahner refers to include the argument that it is impossible to believe in a good God when evil and suffering continue to exist in the world. Christianity claims that God is all-powerful and loving – yet evil and suffering continue to exist. So the argument often is – either God can solve the problem of evil and end suffering and he will not (so he is not a God of love), or he is not capable of solving the problem of evil (so he is not all-powerful, so he cannot be God). Furthermore, think of all the wars fought in the name of God and religion – religion itself seems to do more harm than good. People can justify almost anything in the name of religion. So, for many, such arguments are enough to convince them that unbelief is a more honest option than belief.

Questions
1. What kinds of suffering do teenagers have to cope with today?
2. Do these sufferings influence their attitude to faith, to life in general?

Secular Atheism

It was John Wesley (1703-91), the founder of Methodism, who said two hundred years ago that 'wherever riches have increased, the essence of religion has decreased in the same proportion'. It seems that when we have other things to distract us, to absorb our attention, God fades into the background. It's not so much that we come to the conclusion that God does not exist – it's just that there is no room in our life for God. Material wealth, success, sport and sex are all alternative gods in this consumer society. Religion may still be kept for 'special occasions' – birth, marriage, death – but most of the time people are simply too busy living, coping with what they see as the real world, to bother with a God whom they think is part of another world. This is what secularism in its true sense is – the belief that this world is all there is to reality – and that happiness is to be sought and found only in this life. The result is what the Vatican Council described as 'the deadening of the religious question'.

> Some never get to the point of raising questions about God, since they seem to experience no religious stirrings, nor do they see why they should trouble themselves about religion. (*The Church in the Modern World*, 19)

In this sense, it is not so much that people make a deliberate choice not to believe – it is more a 'non-decision' – a total indifference to the idea of God and religion. In an age that emphasises the human, there seems to be little room for the divine.

The search for happiness gives us a further clue to some of the characteristics of this secular age. More than ever before, we are less inclined to put up with pain or difficult situations.

Decisions are frequently made on the basis of 'I like it', or 'I don't feel like it' – thus the emphasis is on the immediate and on the self. Television and advertising paint a picture of success and happiness that is a reversal of the Beatitudes as found in Matthew's Gospel.

> Happy are the glossy people – their bodies will be admired.
> Happy are those with spare cash – for the moment, they will be satisfied.
> Happy are those who live with the latest novelty – they will have fun.
> Happy are the tough ones – they know how to get their way.
>
> *Free to Believe,* Michael Paul Gallagher

This is a world where, as Bishop Donal Murray puts it, 'the pursuit of happiness tends to become separated from the idea of moral responsibility'. A Concern volunteer nurse described her feelings when she returned from Ethiopia via London after the 1984 famine – 'the wealth, the waste – it was just incredible'. There is such an emphasis on 'personal fulfilment' that the other is forgotten. The result is a world where those who do not attain material success fall by the wayside. The unemployed, the homeless, the travellers and the poor often become forgotten victims in a society of greed. If religious faith fades away for those who are too preoccupied by their material world, it becomes simply too difficult for a hopeless people who feel isolated, rejected and abandoned. Theirs is the aimless experience of the Beatles' 'Nowhere Man'.

> He's a real nowhere man
> Sitting in his nowhere land
> Making all his nowhere plans for nobody.
> Doesn't have a point of view
> Knows not where he's going to.

Questions
1. 'People are basically selfish.' Is this a fair comment?
2. What causes people to be selfish?
3. What moves people to concern? What would move you to concern?
4. Does an increase in wealth mean a decrease in faith?

Faith is difficult without some experience of hope. Alienated from the other structures in society, it's not surprising that many feel cut off from the Church too.

False Images of God

In his book *God of Surprises* Gerard Hughes paints the following picture of God which was created in his imagination.

God was a family relative, much admired by Mum and Dad, who described him as very loving, a great friend of the family, very powerful and interested in all of us. Eventually we are taken to visit 'Good Old Uncle George'. He lives in a formidable mansion, is bearded, gruff and threatening. We cannot share our parents' professed admiration for this jewel in the family. At the end of the visit, Uncle George turns to address us. 'Now listen, dear', he begins, looking very severe, 'I want to see you here once a week, and if you fail to come, let me just show you what will happen to you'. He then leads us down to the mansion's basement. It is dark, becomes hotter and hotter as we descend, and we begin to hear unearthly screams. In the basement there are steel doors. Uncle George opens one. 'Now look in there, dear', he says. We see a nightmare vision, an array of blazing furnaces with little demons in attendance, who hurl into the blaze those men, women and children who failed to visit Uncle George or to act in a way he approved. 'And if you don't visit me, dear, that is where you will most certainly go', says Uncle George. He then takes us upstairs again to meet Mum and Dad. As we go home, tightly clutching Dad with one hand and Mum with the other, Mum leans over us and says 'And now don't you love Uncle George with all your heart and soul, mind and strength?' And we, loathing the monster, say 'Yes I do', because to say anything else would be to join the queue at the furnace. At a tender age religious schizophrenia has set in and we keep telling Uncle George how much we love him and how good he is and that we want to do only what pleases him. We observe what we are told are his wishes and dare not admit, even to ourselves, that we loathe him.

Questions and exercises
1. When you think about God, what images come into your mind?
2. What kind of a God would you like to believe in?
3. 'God made men and women in his image and they have got even with him' (Voltaire). What does this statement mean?
   Do you agree with it?

Such is an image of God that may well be of a different age, but there are many such images of God as the following exercise will show.

1. In the first column tick the statement(s) you identify with.

2. In the second column indicate which concept of God each statement reflects: e.g. an angry God; an all-powerful being; a loving father, a supernatural power: a God who sends suffering as a punishment for sin; a remote God – distant from the world and from ordinary people; a just judge, someone to be called on when we can't cope with life ; a God whose attitude towards us depends on our behaviour; a Creator God.

Statements

1. The doctors say there's no hope but God spoke first.		
2. I know it's not true, but I always feel that God stops loving me when I do wrong.		
3. I really believe that God cares about me and sometimes I feel very close to him.		
4. What did I do to deserve this cross? I never did any harm to anyone.		
5. One thing that frightens me about dying is the thought of meeting God – after all the times I've done wrong.		
6. I believe that God made us, God loves us, God wants us to be happy.		
7. I only think of God or pray when I'm really worried or need something badly.		
8. To me, God is not like a person, but some Force behind the Universe.		
9. God is the one who will judge me when I die – but I know that he is fair.		
10. I believe in God but I pray to St Anthony; he never lets me down.		

3. Which of these images of God do you believe in most strongly?
   Which image would you like to believe in?
   Which image do you think most people believe in?

The following is a summary of some of the main images of God that prevail.

1. The great but absent-minded inventor: the one who made everything, passed it on, and then forgot about it.

2. The nice old person: pleasant-natured but old-fashioned, out of touch: can't really cope with the modern world and is no longer relevant; a bit like Santa Claus: nice to tell the children about, but not really important.

3. Superspy: the ultimate in spy satellites who is watching each one of us all the time in order to record our sins and eventually punish us.

4. The artist: made some lovely things; trees, flowers, little furry animals, all really nice to look at.

5. The shoulder: always there in time of trouble or when we need something (also known as the soft touch).

6. The puppeteer: pulls the strings and makes us sit, stand, jump, lie down etc.; completely in control. Be nice to the puppeteer or you're likely to find the strings being cut.

7. The show-off: performs the odd miracle now and again but that's all.

8. The absentee landlord: not really interested in the property; visits occasionally; sometimes helps tenants with their problems; sometimes evicts them without mercy.

9. The equaliser: punishes all wrong-doing quickly, effectively and sometimes in very dramatic ways affecting large groups of people.

10. The executive: efficient, hard-working, but much too busy to see people individually; couldn't possibly give you an appointment.

Questions
1. Which of these images of God, in your opinion, is the most accurate?
2. Do you think people's image of God changes as they go through life? Explain.

In many instances the image of God that people may be rejecting is not God at all – certainly not the God of Christianity. The image of God that people sometimes have does not do justice to their intelligence or humanity. However, in rejecting such an image of God they tend to reject God altogether, as we can see in Pauline's statement:

> I've no time for anything to do with religion any more. And don't tell me I'm just angry with the Church and perhaps I deep-down believe in God still. I hate the God I was given, partly because he made me so silly for so long. I used to be very frightened of sin and all that, until I was about sixteen. Even went to prayer meetings every week at that stage. But I don't want to sound bitter, because really I feel calm about it all now. I'm fully convinced that I've become a better human being since I let go of the crutch of God. I just feel sorry for so many people cramping their lives because they're afraid of that repressive God.
>
> *Help my Unbelief,* Michael Paul Gallagher

Conclusion
In this chapter, we have looked at the forms that unbelief can take.

TYPES OF UNBELIEF	CAUSES		RESULTS	
1. Church Atheism	a.	Disappointment with one's experience of Church	a.	People still practise but feel dissatisfied.
	b.	An image of the the Church as interfering with and limiting human freedom	b.	People reject Church and may also reject God.
	c.	An image of the Church as irrelevant to the concerns of the modern world.	c.	People resent and reject some or all of the Church's teachings.
	d.	An experience of believers as unChristian.	d.	Sometimes people leave the Church of their upbringing to join religious cults.
2. Psychological Atheism	a.	A person may be hurt by or disappointed in people.	a.	If one cannot believe in people it is much more difficult to believe in God.
	b.	The existence of evil and suffering in the world.	b.	How can a good God permit evil/suffering to exist?
	c.	Inhuman acts carried out in the name of religion.	c.	God/religion are rejected because of actions associated with them.
3. Intellectual Atheism	a.	Philosophical conclusion that God does not exist cf. Feuerbach, Camus, Nietzsche.	a.	A well-thought-out rejection of God – a fairly rare experience in this country.
	b.	Scientific thinking – God is no longer needed to explain the world.		
4. Secular Atheism	a.	Materialism	a.	God fades into the background.
	b.	experience of unemployment, poverty, hopelessness	b.	– The individual is concerned only with his or her own happiness and only with the material world. – The individual feels alienated from all structures in society, including the Church. – The individual is indifferent to the whole religious question.
5. False Images of God	a.	Childhood images of God carried over into adulthood.	a.	In rejecting what has rightly become an unacceptable image of God for them, some people reject God altogether.
	b.	Lack of education into a more mature image of God.		
	c.	One's experience of people sometimes affects one's image of God.		

Thus, as we have seen, the story of unbelief and its causes is a complex one. It ranges from complete atheism ('Theos' = God: 'theism' = belief in God: 'atheism' = non-belief in God), to agnosticism ('gnosis' = knowledge: 'gnostic' = one who knows: 'agnostic' = one who does not know), to religious indifference (total apathy to the whole religious question). People may be at different points on the ladder of unbelief (and belief) in their lives – but it is strongly argued that religious indifference is the most common version of unbelief in the western world today.

CHAPTER 3

Why do people believe?

This chapter declares that it is people who think, feel and live who also believe. In this country we have been born into a tradition of faith. Some might argue that faith has been forced upon us. Thus this chapter considers people who arrived at faith through their own capacity to wonder – Plato (BC), Aquinas (through the wonders of creation), Solzhenitsyn (amidst the atheistic Soviet system).

We also examine those who have reflected on the experience of love as a pointer to God (Pascal, Marcel, St Augustine).

Finally, we also consider how the justice question, the question of conscience and people's experience of good in others, point them towards God.

Introduction

Picture the following scenes.

1. Cave dwellers in western Europe 35,000 years ago are burying one of the children of their tribe, taking pains to arrange the body in a deliberate pattern and adorning it with special ornaments and pigmentation.

2. An aged ascetic in India sits quietly in contemplation at the edge of a forest.

3. A Buddhist monk in Sri Lanka walks effortlessly along a pebbled pathway meditating in a monastery garden.

4. A prophet in ancient Israel announces the coming of the 'Day of the Lord'.

   What is Religion? John F. Haught

41

Question

1. What do these four scenes have in common?

Despite what was described in the previous two chapters as the 'decline in faith', there is still a large amount of religious activity going on in the modern world. Whether one believes or disbelieves, it is a fact that religious faith and practice have been part of the history of humankind from earliest times to the present day.

Archaeologists have found evidence in early graves that religious awareness already existed in Neanderthal tribes who roamed the earth between 100,000 and 50,000 years ago. They conclude from carefully arranged rocks and stones that some form of worship took place. More recently, the study of aboriginal tribes in Australia, and other cultures which have remained mostly untouched by modern civilisation, shows various rites of worship.

Stag hunt. Cave painting from Spain.

So, from the beginning, people were not just concerned with food and work and shelter. Something in us caused us to look beyond ourselves to something greater. Why was this so? Even today we can ask: What are people looking for when they turn to religion? What good does religion do? Does it make people happier than they would otherwise be? These are some of the questions we will deal with as we look for an answer to the question, 'Why do people believe?' Just as there are many reasons why people do not believe, there is a variety of complex reasons why people believe. **To begin with, faith is a human activity, and so, to understand why people believe, it is necessary to understand human nature itself, because it is the person who thinks, feels and acts who believes.**

In this country, most of us have been born into some context of faith. In fact, we might sometimes feel that faith has been forced upon us and at times we might wonder what our attitude to faith would be if we had been born into a different situation.

Questions
1. Why do people believe in God?
2. Examine the reasons you have given. Would you admire a person for believing in God for these reasons?

Down through history there have been people who have come to the idea of something greater than themselves through their own ability to think and to ask questions, through their capacity to feel deeply or through their concern for the lives of their fellow human beings. So we will now take a look at some people who have arrived at the idea of God
1. through the mind (Plato, St Thomas Aquinas, Solzhenitsyn)
2. through the heart (Pascal, Frankl, Marcel)
3. through conscience (Mother Teresa, Martin Luther King, 'The Boat People's Saint')

The Mind's Search for God

We think.

> Man is but a reed, the most feeble thing in nature; but he is a *thinking* reed. The entire universe need not arm itself to crush him. A vapour, a drop of water suffices to kill him. But if the universe were to crush him, man would still be more noble than that which killed him, because *he knows* that he dies and the advantage which the universe has over him; the universe knows nothing of this.
>
> *Pensées* 349 – Pascal

We think, we know, we ask questions. This is the basic difference between humanity and the rest of creation. We know and if we do not know, we seek to find out. Once a child begins to talk, conversation becomes a stream of questions. The grown person too asks questions and sometimes these questions are greater than any answer that we can find. Such questions concern our very existence. They are questions of meaning – the meaning of one's world and one's life. They are questions that have occupied the minds of the greatest thinkers down through history. They are questions that raise the possibility of a supreme being, a God, as the source of meaning for all of Creation.

Questions
1. Human beings ask questions. Are there some questions which are difficult to answer? Explain.
2. What do you think are some of the deeper questions of life?
3. Is it important
   a. to have philosophers in society?
   b. to be philosophers ourselves?

A philosopher is one who stands back from life and asks major questions about what life is all about. In one sense we are all philosophers. Most days we get on with the business of living but sometimes we do ask bigger questions about our own lives and, indeed, about life in general. Down through the ages there have been those who spent much time considering the meaning of life. Through their search for meaning they have come to believe in some kind of an absolute – a god as the source of all meaning. Here we will consider the ideas of three philosophers in particular.

a. Plato, who dates from before the time of Christ
b. Thomas Aquinas, a philosopher of the Middle Ages
c. Alexander Solzhenitsyn, a modern-day philosopher

a. Plato

The Greek philosopher Plato was born in Athens around the year 428 BC. His was a noble family and it was expected that he would follow a career in the politics of Athens, but instead he became a philosopher – why such a change in career plan? Plato himself, in a letter written in 353 BC, explains:

> When I was young I felt like so many others: as soon as I should become my own master, I thought, I would immediately enter public life. But my way was crossed by certain events in the affairs of the polis [city].

The Greek philosopher, Plato, with his disciples in the garden of the Akademia

These 'events in the affairs of the polis' were the series of corrupt governments that Plato witnessed in the city of Athens. As a young man he had expected the rulers to be just and fair, but what he experienced was corruption at every level. He lost the desire to become involved in such politics himself and instead spent his life considering how the situation could be improved. His conclusion was that only the right philosophy could enable one to know what was right in the polis and in the life of the individual. Furthermore, there would be no justice in the polis until the philosopher became the ruler. The philosopher's rule would be good because such a person has a knowledge of the virtues of wisdom, courage, temperance and justice. Plato then went on to say that something more was required. The ruler should have a knowledge of the *agathon* – the good – which is the highest form of knowledge. It is from the *agathon* that all the virtues and all the forms of knowledge are derived, and it is towards the good that the soul reaches.

What is the idea of the *agathon*?
Plato's answer is that nothing at all can be said about the content of the *agathon*. It is greater than any explanation that we can give. It is 'the cause of knowledge and of truth' but it is greater than them. It is transcendent. One can describe a child of the *agathon* but one cannot describe the good itself!

Here in the philosophy of Plato, almost 400 years before the birth of Christ, we find the idea of something greater than human wisdom – something transcendent, the *agathon*.

This idea of the good is what Plato sees as giving meaning to all human virtues and forms of knowledge. It is, ultimately, what gives meaning to our lives and what enables us to live in justice and peace.

Questions
1. Do you agree that the highest form of knowledge is 'the good'?
2. How can goodness give meaning to our lives?

b. St Thomas Aquinas (1225–74)

Thomas Aquinas was born near Naples in Italy in 1225. At the age of five he was sent to the Benedictine Abbey of Monte Casino to be educated. He then went on to the University of Naples where he studied arithmetic, geometry, grammar, logic, music and astronomy. It is said that as a child he was so big and so quiet that his classmates nicknamed him the 'Dumb Ox'. His family thought that he was a dunce but he would prove to be one of the greatest thinkers of all time. He himself said with great humility and gratitude towards God: 'I understood every page I ever read'.

Aquinas' great interest was the study of God. It is said that the only question he ever asked in class was 'What is God?' and he was to spend his lifetime seeking an answer to this question. He believed that by using the human mind to study the created world we could become certain about the existence of God.

At times it is said that in the past people had a kind of blind faith. They simply believed without question or doubt or without feeling the need to make sense of their faith. Aquinas, though he lived in the Middle Ages at the height of Christianity, was not one of these people. Instead he wanted to show that faith was reasonable, that in the light of our experience in the world it made sense to believe in God.

Exercise
Give examples of 'blind faith'.

Aquinas first considered the facts of human experience – our experience of our own human nature, our experience of others and our experience of the universe. Even as we consider such experiences it becomes obvious to us that there are many unanswered questions. Unlike Aquinas we have the benefit of much scientific knowledge, yet we can still ask:

- Why should human beings exist at all?
- Why should the universe be intelligible rather than chaotic?
- Why are some people good and others evil?
- How do we account for beauty? Is it the mere arrangement of atoms?
- How would you answer these questions?

> It was questions like these which prompted Aquinas' so-called Five Proofs of the Existence of God. These are not 'proofs' in the way we might understand proof as scientific evidence. Rather they are five ways of coming to believe in God. They are 'proofs' founded on the experience of living in the world.
>
> *The Mystery of God*, Teacher's Book

The five proofs of God's existence

1. The proof from motion
This proof considers movement in the world. Everything that moves or changes is being moved by something else. Somewhere there must a source of all motion, a First Mover, who is God.

2. The proof from cause and effect
We see things around us that are being caused by other things, and these other things are being caused by other things again. Eventually we must come to a First Cause, God, who is not caused by anything else.

3. The proof from existence

Everything in the world depends for its existence on something else. Sooner or later we must come to someone who does not depend for existence on someone else, someone who is the reason for his or her own existence. This someone is God.

4. The proof from the qualities of goodness, truth and excellence

There must be somebody who is the cause of these qualities and who is good and true and excellent in the highest degree.

5. The proof from the order and purpose in the world

There must be a Supreme Intelligence who maintains this order and causes the whole of creation to work together for the smooth running of the universe.

The Mystery of God, Teacher's Book

Exercise

1. Give examples of each of the proofs of God's existence.

c. Alexander Solzhenitsyn

Alexander Solzhenitsyn was born in Russia in 1918, a year after the revolution. So he was part of the first Soviet generation to grow up under Communism. His education was typical of the atheistic education of the time and he grew up supporting the philosophy on which Communism was based. He fought with the Red Army in the Second World War, but while serving as an artillery officer in 1945 he was arrested on the charge of criticising Stalin in a personal letter which he had written to a friend. He was sentenced to eight years' penal servitude in a labour camp. This was to be the most crucial experience of his life. He entered prison a loyal and convinced Communist. He left prison a vocal and sincere Christian.

While we may well be cynical about such seemingly dramatic 'conversions', it is interesting to discover how this man's transformation took place. His 'conversion', so to speak, was the result of his deep spiritual experiences in prison rather than any instruction he was given on Christian faith. Here was a man for whom faith was born from within himself and from his experience of life in prison and for which he was truly grateful.

> I nourished my soul there, and I say without hesitation: 'Bless you, prison, for having been in my life!'
> *Gulag Archipelago II*

He was to use this experience and the insights it gave him to bear witness to the fate of millions who suffered in the 'Gulag Archpelago', and to attack what he now considered to be the evils of the 1917 Revolution.

Alexander Solzhenitsyn and his wife, Natalia, at Heathrow Airport, London, in 1983

After leaving prison, he wrote his first novel, *One Day in the Life of Ivan Denisovitch*, which was published in Moscow in 1962. It described the forced labour camps which were part of Stalin's industrial policy. He went on to produce two further novels, *First Circle* and *Cancer Ward*, which were rejected by the Russian censors because of their criticisms of Stalin and the Soviet system.

However, these novels were highly regarded in the west and, in 1974, Solzhenitsyn was awarded the Nobel Prize for Literature. He was by now proving very embarrassing to the Soviet authorities but they were afraid to imprison him because of his prestige in the west. Instead they expelled him from the Soviet Union in 1974. He continued to write, producing works like *The Gulag Archipelago* and *Candle in the Wind*.

Question
Does the experience of suffering make people think? Always? Why?

Solzhenitsyn's philosophy

Solzhenitsyn's philosophy was mostly born out of his experience of life in Soviet Union. Three experiences, the labour camp, war and cancer provided powerful insights for this influential novelist whose ideas are intended for everyone. His achievement is a most remarkable witness to the spiritual mystery of the person. It points towards that 'spark of transcendence' which raises the human person above all history, all politics and even the whole universe. Confined as he was to prison, his spirit rose above his situation and the communist system which had imprisoned him.

It is true that not everyone who undergoes an experience similar to that of the labour camps emerges transformed as Solzhenitsyn was. It is equally true that people can come to the idea of something greater than themselves – something transcendent – without undergoing such a horrific experience. Yet sometimes it takes a kind of 'shock treatment' for us to discover what really matters. Solzhenitsyn puts it like this:

> And thus it is that we have to keep getting banged on the flank and snout again and again so as to become, in time at least, human beings, yes human beings.

In this way the ideas we hold are tested by life until we arrive at the truth by which we can live.

The ultimate question, which Solzhenitsyn borrows from his fellow countryman and novelist, Leo Tolstoy (1829-1910), is 'What is it which makes men live?'

He addresses this question in his novel *Cancer Ward*. One of the characters, Dyoma, a studious youth, conditioned by his education in the wonder of science, answers: 'in the first place air – then water – then food.'

Another character in the novel, an unscrupulous man, Yefrem Podduyev, has relied upon his own strength for years but now has cancer of the throat and is forced to give some thought to deeper questions. He once would have given the same answer as Dyoma to Tolstoy's question, only he would have said vodka instead of water. Up to the time of his illness everything had been crystal clear for him. What counted was work and what he could earn. This held true, it holds true for everyone as long as we do not know we are going to die. Then, unless we want to hide from the truth as many people do, we have to admit that we have neglected 'something'. Podduyev realises that work, the fatherland, the interests of society are all sources of meaning for us, while we are still alive and part of society – but only while we are alive. We die alone. Death strips us of everything that is less than ourselves. The thought of death causes the mind to focus on what is essential. For Solzhenitsyn it raises the question of ultimate meaning, that same question posed in Luke's Gospel where the man storing up provision for a whole year does not know if he will survive until evening.

> So soon as a man falls into affliction the question takes hold and goes on repeating itself incessantly. Why? Why? Why? Christ himself asked it: Why hast thou forsaken me?
>
> There can be no answer to the 'why' of the afflicted, because the world is necessity and not purpose. If there were finality in the world, the place of the good would not be in the other world. Whenever we look for final excuses in this world it refuses them. But to know that it refuses, one has to ask.
>
> The only things that compels us to ask the questions are affliction, and also beauty; for the beautiful gives us such a vivid sense of the presence of something good that we look for some purpose there without ever finding one. Like affliction, beauty compels us to ask: Why? Why is this thing beautiful? But rare are those who are capable of asking themselves this question for as long as a few hours at a time. The afflicted man's question goes on for hours, days, years; it ceases only when he has no strength left.
>
> He who is capable not only of crying out but also of listening will bear the answer. Silence is the answer.... He who is capable not only of listening but also of loving hears this silence as the word of God.
>
> *Gateway to God,* Simone Weil

Warning to the western world

While Solzhenitsyn was deeply critical of what the Communist system was doing to people in the east he was not too impressed by what he found in the so-called 'developed' and 'free' societies of the west. In chapter 2, we saw some of the characteristics of these 'developed' societies where the use of secular materialism caused God to fade into the background as we concerned ourselves with our own individual happiness in a material world.

In an interview on the BBC television programme *Panorama*, in 1976, Solzhenitsyn said that he considers himself a critic of the weakness of the west. As an exile from Russia, the east, he cannot understand 'how one can lose one's spiritual strength, one's will-power and, possessing freedom not value it, not be willing to make sacrifices for it'.

In a broadcast on BBC radio in the same year he pinpoints the selfishness of a society without spiritual values.

> Since there are no higher spiritual forces above us and since I – Man with a capital M – am the crowning glory of the universe, then should anyone have to perish today, then let it be someone else, anybody but not I, not my precious self, nor those who are close to me.

In his play *Candle in the Wind*, published in 1974, his tone is more hopeful.

> What I should like to do is make sure the flickering candle of our soul stays alight till it reaches one more witness. The essential thing is that it should not be snuffed out in our century, in this century of steel and the atom.

Questions
1. What do you like about Solzhenitsyn's last statement?
2. What does Solzhenitsyn mean by 'the flickering candle of our soul'?
3. Has the 'flickering candle of our soul' been snuffed out as we approach the end of the twentieth century?
4. What closes people's eyes to deeper issues?

The Heart's Search for God

We are not just thinking beings whose whole reason for living can be satisfied by thought alone. We feel, we hunger, we love. It is within this human experience of hunger and of love that we find another clue to why we believe. Here, a different kind of logic prevails. In chapter 1, we saw the emphasis that the philosophers of the Enlightenment put on reason. We learned that those things that could not be proven by human reason alone were questioned. We saw that the existence of God was doubted because it could not be scientifically proven. In this chapter we ask: Are reason and science the only forms of truth?

Perhaps one of the most famous challenges to the exclusive authority claimed by reason and science comes from the French philosopher, Blaise Pascal. As a mathematician, engineer and physicist, Pascal had great respect for the scientific method but was equally convinced that there was another form of truth.

Pascal and the Logic of the Heart

Blaise Pascal was born in Clermont in France in 1623, the son of a government official. His was a short life, but by the time he died in 1662, he had left his mark on mathematics, physics, religious thinking and literature. Here was someone who, at twelve years of age, worked out the basic laws of geometry. At nineteen he wrote an essay on conic sections which became known as 'Pascal's Theorem'. By the time he was twenty-three he had discovered atmospheric pressure, invented the hydraulic press and the first calculating machine for his father, a busy tax commissioner.

Pascal had great respect for reason but he also recognised intuition. He valued the intellect but he was drawn by simple affection. He had nothing against logic but believed also in instinct. It is within this other 'realm of truth' – intuition, simple affection and instinct – that love is felt and that belief in God becomes a possibility. For Pascal, the proof of God's existence lay not so much in the created world as in the hunger of the human heart.

> The heart has its reasons, which reason knows not,
> as we see in a thousand. It is the heart that is conscious of God, and not the reason.
> This then is faith – God sensible to the heart, not to reason.
> *Pensées* 277, 278

Question
1. Why do you think that it is within this 'other realm of truth' that belief in God becomes a possibility?
2. Are there people who are insensitive to 'the logic of the heart'?

For Pascal the heart was not sentiment or feeling, it was rather the most secret part of our being, that which is deepest and truest in us. It knows with no less certainty than the intellect but it is a different kind of knowledge, as illustrated in a story told by a priest giving a retreat.

> I remember directing a retreat in a seminary some time back, when a particular student came to talk about some issues in his own life – and it was a real freedom for him to be able to speak of these personal worries for the first time. He came back the next day with quite different questions, saying that he seemed unable to pray and was wondering what faith is. I asked him whether he remembered our conversation of the previous morning. He replied that he could hardly forget and that it had been important for him in many ways. I then 'pushed' him somewhat: how did he know that I did not 'blab' about his personal life with my fellow retreat directors over dinner? No, he said, he was sure that I had never mentioned anything of what he had spoken about. But he had no idea what I had been talking about over the meal. Still, he answered, he remained certain that I had said nothing about him. 'But you have no proof of that', I countered. 'None', he replied, 'except that I trust you'. 'Thank you', I remember saying, 'that is an act of faith'. That is what faith is like: not having the room bugged, but something akin to trust between persons.
>
> *Free to Believe,* Michael Paul Gallagher

The experience of love as a pointer towards God

The following is the last poem written by the American poet Raymond Carver, before he died of lung cancer.

And did you get what you wanted from
This life, even so?
I did.
And what did you want?
To call myself beloved, to feel myself
Beloved on the earth.

                        'Late Fragment'

Prisoners at Auschwitz concentration camp, Poland, as found by Soviet soldiers in 1944

The experience of loving and of being loved is crucial to human survival and happiness. People can endure almost anything if they feel themselves beloved. One of the best known proofs of such a theory comes from the psychiatrist, Victor Frankl, who was born in Vienna in 1905. He spent the Second World War in concentration camps at Auschwitz and Dachau as prisoner No. 119,104. He tells the story of how he survived these camps in a book called *Man's Search for Meaning*. In it he reveals that it was his wife and their love that kept him alive. He had the following insight marching one morning from the camp to the worksite in the dark and cold, while clinging to an image of his wife.

> A thought transfixed me: for the first time in my life I saw the truth as it is set into song by so many poets, proclaimed as the final wisdom by so many thinkers. The truth – that love is the ultimate and the highest goal to which man can aspire. Then I grasped the meaning of the greatest secret that human poetry and human thought and belief have to impart: *The salvation of man is through love and in love.*

Question
1. Did the concentration camps originate in a denial of God? Explain.

Gabriel Marcel

'The salvation of man is in and through love'. We get a clue as to what Frankl means by this in the writings of the French philosopher, Gabriel Marcel, who was born in Paris in 1889. His mother died when he was four and his father, a well-educated and well-travelled man, highly involved in cultural affairs, married an aunt of Gabriel's who raised the young boy. Marcel said that while he only vaguely remembered his mother, he felt her presence with him throughout his life.

This feeling may help to explain the idea that he was to put forward in his writings – that the visible is not the only world. There is a part of reality which, though unseen and unprovable (in the scientific sense), can be known through the experiences of fidelity, hope and love. This part of reality has to do with something greater than ourselves, something beyond the here and now, something that survives death, something eternal. This 'something' Marcel calls *being*. We get a glimpse of what is meant by 'being' in the experience of love. Marcel puts it like this: To say that one loves another person is to say 'Thou, at least, shalt not die'. Marcel takes this to mean 'Because I love you, there is something in you which can bridge the abyss that I vaguely call Death'. This may seem a difficult concept to grasp until we begin to reflect on love. Nobody declares true love for another person with conditions attached. The idea of 'forever' is built in to our expectations of love. There is the belief, the hope that neither the tests of time nor the power of death can destroy such love. In the experience of love, we feel uplifted, fulfilled, pushed beyond the confines of ourselves and of time. This is why Marcel regards the experience of love as well as that of fidelity and hope as access points to something eternal, to God. It is what leads him to adopt the words of the novelist, E.M. Forster, 'It is the personal life and it alone which holds up the mirror to infinity'.

People in love cannot help speaking of their loved one as divine and adorable and of their love as undying, everlasting, eternal. They cannot help feeling that love comes from beyond themselves and carries them beyond themselves.... The only possible explanation is that, whether we realise it or not, *all human love is finally a longing for God.* Only God can give that timeless happiness, that perfect satisfaction, that unchanging loveableness, that unfailing faithfulness which men and women are seeking in one another's love, but cannot fully find there.

Irish Bishops' Pastoral, *Christian Marriage,* 1969

 Questions
1. What would make you completely happy?
2. What is 'complete happiness'?
3. Is it possible to achieve complete happiness?

The restlessness of the human heart

The First Noble Truth in Buddhist thinking is that *all life is dukkha* (suffering). This truth refers not only to physical suffering but also to that frustration which is part of the human condition – namely the inability to reach a point in our lives when we can say that everything is all right, that life is absolutely perfect, that we are totally happy. Even amidst moments of 'perfect' joy, there is the niggling fear that something will go wrong. Having looked forward to something for so long, there is often a feeling of anti-climax when the moment arrives. Having fulfilled one ambition in our lives, we are still restless and long to move on. Why is life so unsatisfactory? Why are we so full of restless desire that never seems to be satisfied? Why all the constant longing? An answer is given to these questions in the *Confessions* of St Augustine.

St Augustine (354-430)

St Augustine was born at Thagaste in North Africa in 354 AD at a time when the Roman Empire was being destroyed by the barbarian invasions. His mother, Monica, was a Christian. His father Patricius, one of the Roman administrators of the town, remarried a pagan until the year 371 AD. Augustine received a Christian education and when he was sixteen, his father decided to send him to Carthage to become a lawyer. However, it took some months to gather the necessary funds and so Augustine spent almost a year in idleness in Thagaste, where he concentrated on a little 'education' of his own. During this year, 369 AD, he devoted his time to seeking out all the pleasures that seemed so attractive to a sixteen-year-old! At first he prayed (though he did not seem too anxious to have his prayers heard) 'Give me chastity, Lord, but not just yet'. When he arrived in Carthage at the end of the following year, he was ready for every distraction. In this half-pagan city he encountered the free and easy morals of the other students. He loved the theatre and was delighted with his own success at writing. 'I was puffed up with vanity'. He wanted to be the leader, especially in evil deeds. 'I was ashamed not to be shameless'. It was not long before he had to confess that a son had been born to him, 'the son of his sin'.

In 373 AD Augustine's whole life was changed by his reading of the *Hortensius* by the Greek philosopher, Cicero. Cicero advocated Plato's idea, which was to live the life of the philosopher, reach towards the *agathon* and abandon destructive passions. It impressed Augustine.

> This book changed my affections, and it turned my prayers towards Thee, O Lord, and it changed my purposes and desires. With an incredible beat of my heart I yearned for the immortality of wisdom; and I began to rouse myself that I might return to Thee.
>
> *Confessions III, 4*

His conversion was not easy. Augustine was to spend the next fifteen years in anguish and struggle. In the *Confessions*, he describes the restlessness and hunger of his heart. He writes about his desperate search for fulfilment, often in false directions which left him feeling empty and dissatisfied. Why was he so restless? Why could he not find peace? These same questions were asked by the poet W.B. Yeats, over fifteen hundred years later.

> But is there any comfort to be found?
> Man is in love and loves what vanishes,
> What more is there to say?

St Augustine's eventual answer was that only God can satisfy this hunger. The restlessness, the weariness, the longing we experience, is our desire for God.

> You have made us for yourself, O Lord,
> And our hearts are restless, until they rest in
> Thee.

The poet George Herbert comes to the same conclusion as Augustine when he suggests that God deliberately created us with this restlessness, so that we might not become too satisfied with life in this world and lose our desire for God.

> When God at first made man,
> having a glass of blessings standing by,
> let us (said he) pour on him all we can;
> let the world's riches, which dispersed lie,
> Contract into a pin.

> So strength first made a way,
> Then beauty flow'd, then wisdom, honour, pleasure:
> When almost all was out, God made a stay,
> Perceiving that alone of all his treasures
> Rest on the bottom lay.

Then God deprived man of one blessing.

> Yet let him keep the rest,
> But keep them with repining restlessness:
> Let him be rich and weary, that at least,
> If goodness lead him not, yet weariness
> May toss him to my breast.
>   'The Pulley'

Questions
1. Do you ever feel restless or dissatisfied?
2. What do you think causes this?

In December 1984 the BBC pictures of the famine in Ethiopia flashed across the televisions of the western world, just as Christmas was about to be celebrated. For a while, people paused. The story had awakened something deep, something we might even call primitive in the human heart – the call to be generous, to reach out to our fellow human beings who were in pain. That Christmas, one could almost hear a universal chorus chant: 'Something must be done'.

However short-lived such generosity is, at moments like this we experience an innate sense of right and wrong. We experience the urge to look beyond ourselves to the needs of our fellow human beings. At such times, God is experienced as a call to live a more generous life. Instead of arriving at a sense of God through thought or through the hungers of the heart, we glimpse God in the call of conscience. It is this reality that caused Cardinal Newman to declare: 'We believe because we love'.

Questions
1. What prompts you to be good or generous?
2. Why is our generosity often so short-lived?

The experience of injustice, the plight of the oppressed, the hungry and the poor awakens in us an urge to act to restore justice. Even when this urge is short-lived, when it costs too much for us to follow it through, deep down we still know that it is right.

> Even when we ourselves err a hundred times, we cannot be satisfied with a world in which some die of hunger while others suffer from the consequences of their well-being. Evil evokes the judgement that it just can't go on like that. We have to protest. And in that protest there is something unconditioned and no longer questionable.... Injustice and suffering cry out for absolute justice.
> *Introduction to Christian Faith,* Walter Kasper

Such was the cry of President Mary Robinson at a press conference in Nairobi after her visit to famine-stricken Somalia in October 1992.

> We share this world. I have an inner sense of justice that has been offended by what I've seen in the last three days. Deeply offended. I cannot reconcile myself to the fact that I have witnessed directly the queues and the deprivation of people.

a. Mother Teresa

We glimpse something of the absolute which we call God in both the sense of helplessness we ourselves feel and in our cry for absolute justice. We glimpse something of God also in people whose lives are dedicated to relieving injustice wherever they find it. When Mother Teresa visited Ireland in June 1993, a young mother from Ballymun commented,

'God, she'd make you believe in God, wouldn't she!' *Irish Independent* , 4 June 1993.

In his autobiography, *The Time of my Life,* Gay Byrne describes his TV interview with Mother Teresa in 1973.

> I find it hard to describe the effect she had on me. Interviewing her was like looking into a bowl of shining light. The audience that night was also deeply affected, and unbidden during the break, they passed around the only receptacle they could find – some lad's motorcycle helmet – and filled it with money, engagement rings, everything they could give.

This interview was to be the turning-point in the life of carpenter Eamon Butler, who followed her to India. He describes his experience as he walked into her home for the dying in Calcutta.

> I felt a special grace which has helped me to cope with what I saw. Within a week, I was able to hold dying people, wash the dead, something I could never have dreamed of. Now I have seen death in a different light – as a rebirth, as life after going home, as the final stuff.

There are others too for whom the sense of God finds expression in their attempt to relieve injustice.

b. Martin Luther King

On 28 August 1963, at the Lincoln Memorial in Washington DC, before a crowd of a quarter of a million, sixty thousand of them white, a crowd that included personalities like Marlon Brando, Charlton Heston and Joan Baez, Martin Luther King, Junior, delivered the following speech:

> I have a dream. It is a dream rooted in the American dream. I have a dream that one day this nation will rise up and live out the true meaning of its creed: 'We hold these truths to be self-evident that all men are created equal'.

> I have a dream that one day on the red hills of Georgia, sons of former slaves and sons of former slave-owners will be able to sit down together at the table of brotherhood.

I have a dream that one day even the State of Mississippi, a state sweltering with the heat of injustice, will be transformed into an oasis of freedom and justice.

I have a dream that one day my four little children will live in a nation where they will not be judged by the colour of their skin, but by the content of their character. I have a dream that one day every valley shall be exalted, every hill and mountain shall be made low. The rough places will be made plain, and the crooked places will be made straight. This is the faith that I go back to the South with. With this faith, we shall be able to hew out of the mountain of despair, a stone of hope. With this faith we will be able to work together, to pray together, to struggle together, to go to jail together, to stand up for freedom together, knowing we will be free one day.

This will be the day when all of God's children will be able to sing with new meaning 'let freedom ring'. So let freedom ring from the prodigious hilltops of New Hampshire. Let freedom ring from the mighty mountains of New York. But not only that. Let freedom ring from the stone mountains of Georgia. Let freedom ring from every hill and molehill of Mississippi, from every mountainside.

When we allow freedom to ring – when we let it ring from every city, we will be able to speed up that day when all God's children, black men and white men, Jews and Gentiles, Protestants and Catholics, will be able to join hands and sing in the words of the Negro spiritual: 'Free at last, free at last, Great God Almighty we are free at last'.

These are the words of a man whose country professed 'inalienable rights' for all her citizens but still had segregated hospitals and schools and city buses with 'white only' sections.

They are the words of a man who denounced Communism because in denying the existence of God, in denying our spiritual dimension, it called on us to be our own saviour, our own redeemer. History had proved what a doomed task this was.

These are the words of a man whose motivation was Christian and whose methods were peaceful. 'From my Christian background I gained my ideals and from Gandhi my operational techniques'.

They are the words of a man who, though fighting for civil rights for blacks, also professed, 'But I know that justice is indivisible, injustice anywhere is a threat to justice everywhere'.

They are the words of a man whose efforts to liberate his fellow blacks cost him the ultimate price – his life – on the balcony of a Memphis hotel on 4 April 1968 from a gunshot wound in the neck.

Questions and exercises
1. Pick out the lines in Martin Luther's King's speech which mean the most to you and explain why.
2. What inspired Martin Luther King?

c. The Boat People's Saint

Most of the people whose lives are devoted to others are not famous as Martin Luther King and Mother Teresa are. Rather they live quiet lives of goodness and are only known and appreciated by those who encounter them directly. One such person is the 'Boat People's Saint'. We do not even know her name. Indeed we would probably not even know about her at all but for the influence she had on John Redmond, a Dubliner who was senior platform supervisor with Esso Australia. He was in charge of 'Tinggi A', one of twenty-one oil and gas platforms in the South China Sea. He had heard many stories of the Boat People making their dangerous journeys from Vietnam. One night he encountered them for himself. He tells the story himself and, in particular, highlights the effect their leader had on him.

> At five thirty one morning, a small boat of Vietnamese refugees pulled up alongside the oil platform where John Redmond was in charge. The people in the boat begged for food and drink. When Redmond went to view the scene he noticed, amongst the crowd of fifty-two, the face of the woman he was later to describe as the 'Boat People's Saint'.
>
> Food and drink were given to the refugees but they were not allowed on board the platform until it became clear that they were drowning. They had no belongings.

'Nothing! Except for the threadbare clothes they wore, these people had not a single possession. A product of our consumer-orientated society, I could not at first believe that that was possible.' They did not even have shoes.

The crew of the oil rig proceeded to supply the refugees with rubber matting so that they could be made more comfortable. All through the attempts to organise the people, the woman seemed to have been their natural leader. At all times she quietly saw to everyone's needs while forgetting about her own. She went without food or room on the matting until it became available. As evening approached, 'she was still going from one to the other seeing to their needs, moving them closer together so that the ones on either end of each group were also protected.' Finally she was so weakened that she fainted. 'I was deeply concerned for her well-being, for I was convinced that she found an inner strength to carry her and her people through their ordeal and having given all, she had little left to carry on.'

Finally, the refugees had to leave the oil platform and continue on their dangerous journey seeking refuge. 'As she lay on the stretcher on the deck, I had a few moments alone with her. She took my hand in both of hers and smiled.....

'The message I received was that she had set out to do something and was happy in its achievement whatever the cost.... I never saw her again.'

The lives of people like Mother Teresa, Martin Luther King and 'The Boat People's Saint' testify to something deeper in us. In a material world, in an age that professes progress beyond one's wildest dreams, they serve as a reminder that the dream has not come true for everyone. They serve as witnesses to the better side of our nature – our generosity and goodness. They sometimes serve as prophets calling forth a noble response in us. They are the kind of people that the poet Brendan Kennelly had in mind in his poem 'The Good'.

The good are vulnerable
as any bird in flight.
They do not think of safety,
are blind to possible extinction
and when most vulnerable
are most themselves.
The good are real as the sun,
are best perceived through clouds
of casual corruption
that cannot kill the luminous sufficiency
that shines on city, sea and wilderness,
fastidiously revealing
one man to another,
who yet will not accept
responsibilities of light.
The good incline to praise,
they have the knack of seeing that
the best is not destroyed
although forever threatened.
The good go naked in all weathers,
and by their nakedness rebuke
the small protective sanities
that hide men from themselves.
The good are difficult to see
though open, rare, destructible;
always they retain a kind of youth,
the vulnerable grace of any bird in flight,
content to be itself,
accomplished master and potential victim
accepting what the earth or sky intends.
I think that I know one or two
among my friends.

Exercise
Kennelly says that he has known one or two really good people in his life.
Consider your life and friends. Identify really good people in your life and describe
the effect they have on you.

Conclusion

In this chapter we considered why people believe in something greater than themselves, in a God. We saw that sometimes belief in God is born out of one's thinking about oneself and one's created world. Sometimes it is the experience of love that points to God and sometimes we glimpse God through our conscience, through our sense of God. So our thoughts, our feelings and our actions can serve as pointers towards something greater than us, as we can see in the chart below.

SUMMARY CHART

1. The mind's search	a. Plato	a. the 'Agathon' or the 'good' gives meaning to everything.
	b. Aquinas	b. five 'proofs' for the existence of God.
	c. Solzhenitsyn	c. poses the question of ultimate meaning: discovers spiritual values.
2. The heart's search	a. Pascal	a. the logic of the heart
	b. Marcel	b. the experience of love as a pointer towards God
	c. St Augustine	c. 'our hearts are restless until they rest in thee.'
3. The call of conscience	a. Mother Teresa	a. 'She'd make you believe in God, wouldn't she?'
	b. Martin Luther King	b. his work for civil rights, for justice
	c. 'The Boat People's Saint'	c. her care for her fellow Vietnamese refugees

Revision questions and exercises

1. Many people's paths to faith have been described in this chapter. Select the one which impresses you most and say why.
2. Which path to faith – the mind's search, the heart's search, or the call of conscience attracts you most? Why?
3. Write an essay entitled 'Why I believe in God'.

'Modern Man in Search of a Soul'

Chapter 4 looks at the modern world and particularly at the issues raised by scientific and technological progress. It identifies that all is not well in this modern world – that human beings have not found happiness to the extent that it was hoped. It recognises that human beings are once again searching for a deeper meaning in their lives and that this time the search is taking the forms of a rise in fundamentalism, a turn to religious cults and the New Age Movement.

The end of the chapter examines the possibility for a turn to religious faith within this modern search for meaning and it suggests that the first step towards faith is the desire to live more fully and more deeply.

Introduction

The title of this chapter is taken from an essay written in 1933 by the psychiatrist Carl Gustav Jung (1875-1961). In it, he considered the plight of people today, caught in a world so different from that of other ages.

> How totally different did the world appear to medieval man! For him the earth was eternally fixed and at rest in the centre of the universe, encircled by the course of the sun... Men were all children of God under the loving care of the Most High, who prepared them for eternal blessedness; and all knew exactly what they should do and how they should conduct themselves in order to rise from a corruptible world to an incorruptible and joyous existence. Such a life no longer seems real to us even in our dreams.

Gone was the security, the certainty that previous generations had enjoyed – but what had replaced it?

As a psychiatrist, Jung had a knowledge of the inner life of 'educated persons, both sick and healthy, coming from every quarter of the civilised white world'. He observed that people were not at ease in this new world. The progress that had been made in science, technology and organisation had not filled the inner void of life, the yearnings and hopes of the soul. As a result, we are now searching for a 'will to live', for something to meet our inner longings, for a spirituality. This search, according to Jung, explained the interest shown in psychology and indeed the 'widespread interest in all sorts of psychic phenomena as manifested in the growth of spiritualism, astrology, theosophy and so forth'.

Carl Gustav Jung (1875-1961)

This suspicion that the external signs of progress have not fulfilled human needs is beginning to take root in many western nations. In the midst of the problems left unsolved, many are becoming increasingly doubtful about the dogma they had believed for so long – 'that science and technology are the key to universal happiness,' and that progress will follow naturally.

There are those who are beginning to doubt whether indeed progress has taken place at all. Perhaps this tale from ancient India sums up the situation of humankind in a scientific and technological world.

Four royal sons were questioning what speciality they should master. They said to one another, 'Let us search the earth and learn a special science'. So they decided and after they had agreed on a place where they would meet again, the four brothers started off, each in a different direction. Time went by, and the brothers met again at the appointed meeting place, and they asked one another what they had learned. 'I have mastered a science', said the first, 'which makes it possible for me, if I have nothing but a piece of bone of some creature, to create straightaway the flesh that goes with it'. 'I', said the second, 'know how to grow that creature's skin and hair if there is flesh on its bones'. The third said, 'I am able to create its limbs if I have the flesh, the skin and the hair'. 'And I', concluded the fourth, 'know how to give life to that creature if its form is complete with limbs'.

Thereupon the four brothers went into the jungle to find a piece of bone so that they could demonstrate their specialities. As fate would have it, the bone they found was a lion's, but they did not know that and picked up the bone. One added flesh to the bone, the second grew hide and hair, the third completed it with matching limbs, and the fourth gave the lion life. Shaking its heavy mane, the ferocious beast arose with its menacing mouth, sharp teeth and merciless claws and jumped on its creators. He killed them all and vanished contentedly into the jungle.

Questions
1. What is the meaning of this tale from ancient India?
2. How can we apply the message of this tale to the modern world?
3. If the brothers in the story had a second chance how could they use their creative powers to make something less dangerous?

For the first time in history we have the power to destroy the world. This power is the product of our own genius but increase in power is not always accompanied by control of that power for the benefit of humanity. The more we know about ourselves and our world, the more uncertain we become.(*Gaudium et spes*, 4)

At another level, the discoveries of science and technology cause us to marvel at the wonders of creation. Consider the following:

Our solar system is part of a huge galaxy of 100,000,000,000 other stars formed into a giant pinwheel in space.

The brain is infinitely more complex than the most modern computer. Within three pounds of flesh – of which 80% is water – it contains from 500–1,000 million specialised cells.

Every individual's thumb or fingerprint is different from that of anyone else.

The realisation that science and technology have not resulted in total human happiness, together with the knowledge that they contain the means of destroying the world as well as causing people to marvel at creation – poses questions for human living, and, indeed, for the possibility of faith.

Question
1. Can you give examples of scientific discovery becoming a threat?

The situation of the human being in the modern world can be considered under the following headings:
1. Science and religion
2. The issues raised by technological progress
3. The search for a new spirituality
4. The first steps towards faith

1. Science and religion

a. The history of the relationship

The relationship between science and religion has had a chequered history. Up to and including the Middle Ages, the Church and the Bible provided the answers to the questions that people raised about themselves and their world. Authority – whether of the Church or the State – was the hallmark of these times and people accepted something as fact on the basis of such authority. The Age of Science changed all of this. From now on, questions of fact were to be settled by experiment and not by authority.

Nicklaus Copernicus

The Age of Science began in the mid-sixteenth century when the Polish priest and astronomer, Nicklaus Copernicus (1473-1543), outlined his ideas in a book called *The Revolutions of Heavenly Spheres*. Having studied the works of Ptolemy, an ancient Egyptian astronomer, he set up his own observatory and studied the movements of the sun, the moon and the stars. From such observation he put forward the idea that the earth moved around the sun and not vice versa as most people believed. In 1608 Dutchman Jan Lippershey invented the telescope, an instrument perfected and used by the Italian astronomer Galileo Galilei (1564-1642). From his observations of mountains and craters on the moon, dark spots on the sun and the moons around the planet Jupiter, Galileo was convinced that Copernicus was right – the earth did revolve around the sun. Such a theory caused problems for the Church because it seemed to contradict biblical statements that the sun rises and sets and circles the earth which was perceived to be stationary (Tb 2:7; Est 11:11). Furthermore, it seemed to play down the Church's belief that the earth was more important than the sun.

Despite the fact that Galileo was able to demonstrate his theory, the Church authorities insisted on belief in what the Bible seemed to say. In 1616 the Holy Office condemned Copernicus' ideas as heretical. Galileo was silenced, his books banned and he himself was placed under house arrest. The stage was now set for the clash between science and religion. Which of these contained the source of truth? Over three hundred years later the words of the American novelist, Pearl S. Buck, would be accepted: 'Science and Religion, Religion and Science, put it as I may, they are two sides of the same glass, through which we see darkly until these two, focussing together, reveal the Truth' (*A Bridge for Passing*, 1962).

The situation was to get worse before it would get better, with faults on both sides. The scientists who continued the work of Galileo plotted the different movements of the sun and the planets. They came up with the idea that the universe resembled a clock and God a clockmaker. As creator, God creates the universe, winds it up and then leaves it to work on its own. Such was the view of the British scientist Sir Isaac Newton (1642-1727), whose three laws of motion accounted for the movements of the heavenly bodies. However, he did realise that there were gaps and irregularities that these laws did not account for. Newton's solution to this problem was to say that God stepped in every now and again to make adjustments, to correct the irregularities. So he would speed up a slowing planet or curb a comet going off course. The problem with such a theory from the point of view of faith was that it created a 'God of the gaps', where God was used to fill the gaps in human knowledge. In time, of course, with increasing scientific discoveries and explanations, there would be less room for God and eventually he would be squeezed out altogether. It was hardly a wonder that the Church had a problem with such scientific thinking.

The nineteenth century saw a further reason for controversy between science and religion when Charles Darwin (1809-1882) put forward the theory of evolution in his book, *The Origin of Species*. Once again, such a theory caused problems for the Church in that it seemed to contradict the biblical view of creation. The Book of Genesis talked about God creating the world in six days. The theory of evolution spoke about gradual development over millions of years. Furthermore, in the early days, many concluded that the theory of evolution implied that we had descended from the ape. Once again, such an interpretation was criticised by the Church, which spoke about the special creation of human beings, different from the rest of creation and endowed with a soul.

As time went on, and according as scientific theories were being backed up by experiment and proof, 'science gradually repainted the pictures of the universe that had informed western minds and hearts for centuries – and deliberately or otherwise, painted God out' (*New Dictionary of Theology*). Science began to represent the more intelligent, the more informed and the more modern view of the world. The Church and some of its teaching was perceived as backward and unintelligent, particularly when the evidence of science was conclusive and contradicted the religious view.

Questions
1. Do you think that it is still true that science represents 'the more intelligent, the more informed and the more modern view of the world'?
2. What is meant by the phrase 'God of the gaps'?

Causes of the problem

The problem concerning the clash between science and religion was twofold.

1. In relation to religion – The Church did not sufficiently take into account the fact that the Bible is not a book of science. The Jews, while having tremendous faith, were a backward people in relation to science. Given that science originated in places outside Israel, in places like Babylonia, Egypt and, later on, Greece, the Bible and its authors were part of a pre-scientific culture. Essentially the Bible is a book of religious faith. When it draws on what we would now consider to be 'themes of a scientific nature' it does so with a view to furthering religious faith. The intent therefore is not scientific teaching but religious teaching. Until well into this century, such a distinction was not drawn and it was thought that every word of the Bible was to be accepted and believed in a literal fashion.

Question
In your opinion, what stories in the Bible are not literally true? Explain.

2. The problem in relation to science was the claim to absolute truth which science was making. Scientific knowledge was seen as the only valid form of knowledge, and other ways of knowing – experience, intuition and faith – were dismissed. Such a narrow view of truth is well expressed by E.F. Schumacher:

> A material scientist is like a man who, although in possession of a radio receiver refuses to use it because he has made up his mind that nothing but atmospheric noises can be obtained from it.

The same point is rather humorously made by Fr Sean Kealy in the introduction to *Science and the Bible:*

> According to the theory of aerodynamics, and as may be readily demonstrated by means of a wind tunnel, the bumble bee is unable to fly. This is because the size, weight and shape of his body in relation to the total wing span make flight impossible. But the bumble bee, being ignorant of these scientific facts and possessing considerable determination, does fly – and makes a little honey too.

Science and religion today

According to Sean Kealy the hostilities between science and religion 'have to a large extent softened'. We have already referred to one of the reasons for this, namely a changed understanding of the Bible. Modern biblical scholarship considers that it is the religious message that is required to be believed in biblical accounts of, for instance, creation. From the point of view of faith, it does not really matter whether the world was created in six days or over millions of years. The essential point of faith is that God created the world. The same principle holds true of many other biblical notions that seemed to be in dispute with science in the past.

From the scientific point of view, there is a growing number of scientists who are beginning to acknowledge, firstly, that there are other forms of truth and, secondly, that the gaps in knowledge that science was trying to fill are becoming wider rather than narrower. Instead of aiming at total knowledge of the universe and its workings, modern scientific discoveries are exposing its complexity and vastness. The American physicist Dr Freeman J. Dyson puts it like this:

Albert Einstein

In physics it turned out that God's creation was far richer than either Maxwell or Einstein had imagined. There was a time in the 1920s and 1930s when it seemed that the landscape was almost fully mapped. The world of physics looked simple. There were the great mountains explored by Maxwell and Einstein and Rutherford and Bohr, the theories of relativity and the quantum, great landmarks standing clear and cold and clean in the sunlight, and between them only a few unimportant valleys still to be surveyed. Now, we know better. After we began to explore seriously the valleys in the 1950s, we found in them flora and fauna as strange as anything to be seen in the valleys of the Amazon. Instead of the three species of elementary particle that were known in the 1920s, we now have sixty-one. Instead of three states of matter – solid, liquid and gas – we now have six or more. Instead of a few succinct equations to summarise the universe of physics, we have a luxuriant growth of mathematical structures, as diverse as the phenomena that they intend to describe. So we have come back to the rain forest, intellectually as well as geographically.

From such a point of view, modern science would seem to be discovering rather than destroying mystery. Scientists are uncovering wonders of the universe about which the biblical writers knew little.

Behind the eye are 130 million light-sensitive rods and cones which cause photo-chemical reactions. These transform light into electrical impulses which are transmitted to the brain at fantastic speed.

Science and the Bible, Sean Kealy

From twenty-three male half-chromosomes and twenty-three female half-chromosomes of two single cells, an embryo is formed. These cells contain not only all the bodily characteristics the human being will possess, but also his entire inheritance from his most remote ancestor.

Mystery of God, Teacher's Book

Perhaps we have more reason than the Psalmist to declare –
O Lord, our Lord, your greatness is seen in all the world (Ps 8:1)
....wonderful are thy works (Ps139:14).

Questions
1. What is the priority of science? What is the priority of religion?
2. Are science and religion compatible? Explain.

2. The issues raised by technological progress

In 1965 Vatican II stated:

In no other age has humankind enjoyed such an abundance of wealth, resources and economic well-being; and yet a huge proportion of the people of the world is plagued by hunger and extreme need while countless numbers are totally illiterate.

Gaudium et spes, 4

It continues:

The human race is growing conscious that the forces it has unleashed are in its own hands and that it is up to human beings to control them or be enslaved by them.

Gaudium et spes, 9

A paper was presented to the 1979 Conference of the World Council of Churches entitled 'Science and Technology – Promises and Threats'.

It first acknowledged the wonderful progress made by science and technology. It talked about technology liberating people from limitations and insecurities.

Medical technology has removed the terror of many diseases and epidemics. Agricultural technologies increase the production of food.... Machines can liberate people from many types of drudgery. They make possible communication, travel, leisure, access to the arts.

Faith, Science and the Future

It then went on to state that despite such promises and developments 'science and technology appear to many people as threats'. This can be seen especially where science affects the natural environment, causing destruction to nature and in turn to human life itself.

> Poor people seeking food and firewood have not intentionally produced dangerous soil erosion but the effect has been disastrous. Households and factories may not intend to pollute the air, but the outcome is as bad as if it were intended. Manufacturers of aerosol cans did not intend to endanger people by depleting the protective ozone in the upper atmosphere, but the unintended happened.
> *Faith, Science and the Future*

It would be foolish not to recognise the very real achievements of science. They have made it possible for the earth to support a larger number of people, enjoying greater wealth, health and leisure than ever existed before. Yet, while we cannot forget the triumphs of modern technology which has ensured that one third of the world is not starving but often overfed, we are becoming aware that, despite the progress, the world is still beset by problems – not just those created by technology itself, but also the human consequences of modern living.

For example; pollution of the environment – air, water, land, the decay of large cities, traffic congestion, homelessness; rising crime and violence, tension between social classes and ethnic groups; the scandal and suffering of large-scale, long-term unemployment, – poverty, the growing gap between rich and poor within the same country and in the world – the sense of helplessness that fills many lives.

We may ask, what is the solution? The scientists Herbert Weiser and H.F. York considered the problems experienced at the height of the international arms race. They observed the reality of what was happening – the contradiction of increasing armaments and decreasing security. They concluded that there was no technical solution to this problem. Rather the solution lay in changing or redirecting human aims and values and human modes of living. This solution applies to many world problems today. It is the same solution proposed by Pope John Paul II in his encyclical *Centesimus annus*.

> It is not wrong to want to live better; What is wrong is a style of life which is presumed to be better when it is directed towards 'having' rather than towards 'being' ...it is therefore necessary to create lifestyles in which the quest for truth, beauty, goodness and communion with others are factors (Par. 36).

Put another way, we can say that to be free from material necessity, to have that which makes life comfortable, should not be an end in itself. Rather, not having to think about food and clothes for tomorrow should provide the means for modern men and women to pursue the higher ends of the good life for themselves and all others.

> Human beings do not live on bread alone, but on every word that comes from the mouth of God. (Mt 4:3; Lk 4:3)

Perhaps this was the fundamental problem with Marxism – the philosophy which proposed a human solution to the problems of humankind.

It was believed, as we saw in chapter 1, that a new world could be brought about by overthrowing the capitalist system and setting up a workers' republic. Marxism contained the promise that happiness could be found within the human and material world. History, particularly recent history, in Eastern Europe has shown what a pipe-dream this was. It is fair to suggest that Marxism has failed because, as Pope John Paul II again says:

> it is not possible to understand man on the basis of economics alone, nor to define him simply on the basis of class membership....Marxism had promised to uproot the need for God from the human heart, but the results have shown that it is not possible to succeed in this without throwing the heart into turmoil. (*CA*, 24)

If science is giving us more reasons to marvel at the wonders of creation, perhaps we can also say that the impotence and unease felt by human beings in a technological world is once again creating the recognition of the need for a saviour.

We have already seen that modern technology is posing basic ecological questions that call for a change in human aims and values.

The net result of the dawning realisation of the limitations of science and technology as ultimate sources of meaning is a search for something beyond the physical – a metaphysics. Ever-increasing numbers of people feel dissatisfaction, frustration and boredom with life in the modern world and yearn for something new. This partly explains the interest in the phenomenon of moving statues, in religious cults, and even sometimes in black magic and forms of satanism. This search for a spirituality, for a soul, takes many forms, and what people are ultimately seeking is equally varied. Where religion is concerned, we find that some abandon the religion they were brought up with for another form of 'spirituality'. Others return to it with a more adult understanding and commitment while others still never knew any formal religion but are now searching for something that will give meaning to their lives.

 Question
Do you agree that science and technology have not resulted in overall human happiness? Explain.

An effort to categorise the trends that the 'spiritual revival' is taking will identify four main groupings.

1. The fundamentalist resurgence

From the cultural/theological point of view, fundamentalism is opposed to religious and cultural liberalism and defends orthodoxy and tradition. It first emerged among American Protestant evangelicals towards the end of the nineteenth century. Essentially it stressed the authority of the Bible and called for clean living. It opposed the theory of evolution and modern studies and interpretations of the Bible. Its hallmark became the literal interpretation of the Scriptures which made no allowance either for better understanding of the context in which the Scriptures were written or for clearer understanding of the mindset of the writers. It also emphasised moral living, usually understood in the narrow sense. Christian fundamentalism is on the increase today for a variety of reasons.

A. In a materialistic and pleasure-seeking world some believe that 'it is only by returning to the religious attitudes and practices of the past that we can stem the rising tide of paganism spreading across the world'. (*Redemptive Intimacy*, D. Westley).

B. The Church since Vatican II is perceived by some as being less certain, less demanding and more liberal. The kind of freedom, the emphasis on conscience, seen to be part of a post-Vatican II Church, is blamed for the decline in Church practice, faith and morals.

Fundamentalism represents a call to return to those tried and true religious postures of a by-gone day, when certainty and strength prevailed and definite demands were made on people.

C. As with political conservatism, extreme religious conservatism (fundamentalism) often replaces liberalism where liberalism is seen to have failed, e.g. the Third Reich (Hitler's totalitarian state) followed the Weimar Republic (a democratic system which failed to solve Germany's problems).

A Nazi rally at Nuremberg, 1933

D. From the individual's point of view, fundamentalism can seem very attractive because people do not have to make decisions about right and wrong. Such decisions are made for them so they cannot be the targets of blame and the burden of freedom is lifted from them. Moreover, at its extreme, almost anything can be justified in the name of God whose will is understood by literal interpretation of the Bible.

Questions
Why do you think that groups like the Jehovah's
Witnesses are on the increase?

2. The appeal of religious cults and sects

The 1960s and the 1970s saw the emergence of many religious cults and sects in the United States. Cults tend to flourish in a society where there is uncertainty, upheaval and crisis. They spread at a time when mainline Churches are experiencing difficulties with falling numbers. A cult can be understood as

> A religious organization founded by and built upon the teachings of a central charismatic figure whose authority is viewed as being equal to or greater than the established scriptures of the major religions. In Christian understanding, the teachings of a cult oppose or differ from historic biblical theology.
> *Understanding the New Age,* Russell Chandler

A sect is a larger religious movement which need not be as closed as a cult.

The main characteristic of a cult is the focus it places on the cult leader. While major historical religious figures such as Moses, Buddha and Muhammad tried to get people to concentrate on something greater than themselves – ultimate mystery, the path to salvation etc., the cult leader usually demands that all the attention be focussed on him. Total loyalty to the leader is often another requirement. Cults tend to be closed off from the wider world of experiences and ideas and turned in on themselves. There is usually an obsession with order and harmony.

> A 'cult' results from the untimely, irrelevant obsession with religious harmony and order when it would be more enlivening to allow individuals in the religious system more autonomy and room for creativity. A cult is the product of a group's clinging to a strong leader's fixed religious ideas about order when the time is ripe for change, diversity and growth.
> *What is Religion?,* J. F. Haught

If cults seem so narrow and closed, what is their appeal, especially for young people? Fr Martin Tierney, in his booklet *Cults, Sects and New Religious Groups,* outlines some of the reasons why people join cults. In a society as diverse and as complex as ours, cults are attractive because of 'their claim to provide simple and indeed simplistic solutions to the most complex problems of life'. There seems to be a solution to every human problem; salvation and happiness are instant. At a very personal level, cults seem to provide 'unconditional acceptance and constant reassurance' for the new member. If there is sadness in a young person's life, the warmth and family atmosphere of a cult can prove irresistible. Moreover, what is seen as the failure of the Churches to meet the needs of young people can drive them into the welcoming arms of the cults. Here they can find order, meaning and harmony, or so it seems. There is an instant family or community experience.

For a generation that professes itself bored with life, cults stem the boredom with constant activity.

> There is something going on from early morning to late at night....your attention is constantly drawn towards things outside yourself, and so you are not in a mental condition to turn inward and reflect; you never get a chance to talk to yourself because there is always somebody else talking to you.
>
> *Cults, Sects and New Religious Groups*

Music, having such appeal, especially for young people, is another attraction. It is not until people are deeply involved in such cults that they may begin to realise the price paid for such a simplistic answer to the meaning of life.

Questions
1. Why do people join cults? What makes them stay?
2. What would you find attractive/unattractive about a religious cult?

3. The New Age Movement

There is general agreement that a new religiosity is emerging in western society. The New Age Movement is seen as the main representative of such a turn to 'religion'. The movement is difficult to define as it is really an umbrella term including phenomena as diverse as astrology and ecology, holistic health and eastern thought. It is described by Fr Jack Finnegan:

> The New Age Movement is an extremely large, loosely structured network of organisations and individuals bound together by common values based on mysticism and Monism (the world view that all is one – man, universe, God), and a common vision of a coming new age of peace and mass enlightenment – the Age of Aquarius.
>
> *New Age Movement* – Tape

The movement is a cultural, and not just a religious movement of western society – the First World. It is the product of a tired culture which has lost its spirituality and is looking for a new one. Old ways of spirituality, e.g. Christianity, are discarded because they are no longer seen as valid in the modern world.

The New Age Movement draws on a whole collection of movements of the past number of decades which include the Consciousness Movement (psychology's belief in the power of the mind), the Ecological Movement, the Women's Movement, the Holistic Health Movement, the Peace Movement, the Metaphysical Movement (which includes the occult and astrology), the Appropriate Technology Movement (which is critical of technology that damages the earth or the environment, e.g. strip-mining), etc.

The central belief behind this movement is that a New Age is emerging. According to Russell Chandler, a journalist with the *Los Angeles Times* who has studied the movement at length, New Agers believe that we are now in the midst of change.

'The limited, finite, Old Order will give way to a glorious, unlimited New Order of peace, prosperity and perfection' (*Understanding the New Age*). This New Order, this New Age is often described as the 'Age of Aquarius', an idea taken from astrology which says that the earth is now entering the Age of Aquarius, having moved out of the Age of Pisces in the 1960s. (An astrological age lasts 2,100 years.) In this New Age, a new 'faith' is emerging

which sees humanity as part of nature – the earth – but having an evolutionary power to go beyond its present state. This attempt to go beyond one's present state is the total responsibility of all of creation. Everything and everyone makes their own history, we create our own salvation – rather than being saved by a redeemer, as is believed in Christianity. Many achieve salvation and perfection through the development of spiritual techniques. Such techniques are drawn from a huge number of sources including Yoga, Zen Buddhism, Celtic religion, astrology, nature religions and magic of every kind.

The New Age Movement is the fastest-growing religious phenomenon in the western world – it is estimated that over ninety million people are involved. It is at one and the same time a rejection of atheistic materialism and of structures and organisations, e.g. Christianity, which are seen as irrelevant, inadequate or oppressive. It seems to be answering that need for a spirituality which is felt by so many people. From a Christian point of view, we will be in a better position to assess its merits and demerits after a study of the Christian concepts of God and of salvation.

Question
What aspects of the New Age Movement can be accommodated in Christianity?

4. The rediscovery of faith – a path to fulfilment

In his book *Stories of Faith*, the American theologian John Shea tells what he calls 'three mini-stories' about different people in different life-settings.

A. 'It was the late afternoon flight from Cleveland to Chicago. Two men were loudly relaxing over drinks. They were dressed in basic business attire and their scarred attaché cases were jammed beneath the seats. The older man was in his late fifties and the younger one around fifty. From the conversation a good guess would be that they were vice-president and sales representative of a small company. They had flown out of Chicago in the morning, made a deal and made it big, and now were on their way back. In the middle of re-hashing their success the older man moved on to a new topic – "This will really make us for the next two years.... You know last winter, Marge and I went down to see Frank and Janice. You remember Frank? He retired about four years ago. They have a nice home right on the golf course outside of Fort Myers. Two bedrooms, just enough. What they do is fly their grandchildren down one at a time – at school breaks and summers – to get to know them. It hit Marge and me that at our age that's what it's all about." '

B. 'A college girl had just returned from a lecture by Mother Teresa of Calcutta. She was impressed...... She now sits cross-legged on the floor of the living room, tracing lines in the perspiration on a Budweiser can and talking with that buoyant confidence that in the next sentence or two everything will come together.

   You know it came to me that people around here are too stuck in themselves. I think that if you went through life and never threw yourself into anything, never found something that you could give yourself to, never go outside yourself, it would be a waste. You have to have a cause. You can't just be doing your own thing.'

C. 'The eighty-three year old man has been dying for about three weeks. For the past two weeks he has been in the hospital. He is conscious about half the time. His son Jim, who is around forty-five, comes each day after work and sits by the bedside. He says he wishes his father would open his eyes so they could talk. But the last time the old man was conscious he called his son Joe and asked him if the ice-wagon was in the neighbourhood. On Friday night just before he left, Jim leaned over to his father, "Oh, Pa, for God's sake let go! Let go! It's got to be better". The old man died early Saturday afternoon. Later Jim told the rest of the family he just knew it was the right thing to say.'

In the film *Shirley Valentine*, Pauline Collins plays the part of a middle-aged housewife whose life as a wife and mother is totally predictable, totally boring and totally for her family. Her friend Jane wins a holiday to Greece and takes Shirley with her. It's the most adventurous thing she has done since she was a teenager. Sitting, sipping wine, looking out at the Mediterranean, she reflects:

I've led such a little life and even that'll be over pretty soon. I've allowed myself to lead this little life when inside me there's so much more and it's all gone unused and now it will never be used. Why do we get all this life if we don't ever use it? Why do we get all these feelings and dreams and hopes if we don't ever use them? That's where Shirley Valentine disappeared to – she got lost in all this unused life.

Questions and exercises
1. In each of these stories the characters had a certain insight into life. Describe each insight.
2. Have you ever had an experience which made you ask what life was all about? Explain.
3. Does religion fade when human living becomes superficial?

The realisation 'That's what it's all about', the declaration 'you have to have a cause', the hope that 'it's got to be better', and the lament of what is seen as an 'unused life', all in the same way pose the question of the meaning of life. It is not a conscious question that enters our life each morning as we awaken.

It is unconscious in that without some element of meaning, we would not continue to live. It only becomes conscious for us at certain times in our lives, at certain key moments of insight. Then it is not as much a question of 'Why get up today?' but a more long-term, ultimate question, 'What is the meaning of life?' 'What is *my* life all about?' At such a moment we awaken to something deep and true in ourselves, something that is often masked by the clutter in our lives. It's almost as if we have two selves – the everyday public, open self and the deeper, private and truer self to which we do not often pay attention. Such is the theme of T.S. Eliot's poem, 'The Love Song of J. Alfred Prufrock' – where 'you and I' represent the 'two selves'. One self is preoccupied with public appearing and daily living:

There will be time, there will be time
To prepare a face to meet the faces that you meet;

My morning coat, my collar mounting firmly to the chin,
My necktie rich and modest, but asserted by a simple pin –

I shall wear the bottom of my trousers rolled.

I have measured out my life with coffee spoons;

In the room the women come and go
Talking of Michelangelo.

The deeper self tries to surface, but with difficulty:

> *Do I dare*
> *Disturb the universe?*
>
> *Should I, after tea and cakes and ices,*
> *Have the strength to force the moment to its crisis?*
>
> *Would it have been worth while,*
> *To have bitten off the matter with a smile,*
> *To have squeezed the universe into a ball*
> *To roll it toward some overwhelming question.*
>
> *I have seen the moment of my greatness flicker.*

It is easier to live at a superficial level, it seems to cost less. It is easier to neglect the deeper part of our humanity and let it go unnoticed for a long time, maybe even forever – but at what price? As one student put it:

> My greatest fear is that I will one day lie on my deathbed and realise that I did not really live life at all.

 Question
What would you like to do before you die so as to avoid deathbed regrets?

How can we avoid such a deathbed regret? How can we discover and really live out of the deeper and more authentic level of our being? In *Free to Believe,* Michael Paul Gallagher writes about the insight that the founder of his order, Ignatius Loyola, had while recovering from a leg injury:

> This story took place in the north of Spain in the year 1521. What happened to one man then set a headline that has influenced thousands of people since; what he experienced and he discovered through his experience became a classic adventure of how to arrive at inner freedom. The man's name was Inigo, and he was a mixture of courtier and soldier; although near thirty years old he had remained a bit of a drifter until this episode opened new horizons for him.
>
> The beginning was nothing extraordinary for a soldier of those times: his leg was broken by a cannon ball in battle and he was carted home to recover if he could. Within a month of the injury he was near death. Then he rallied and managed to survive three grim operations (without anaesthetic). The battle had taken place on

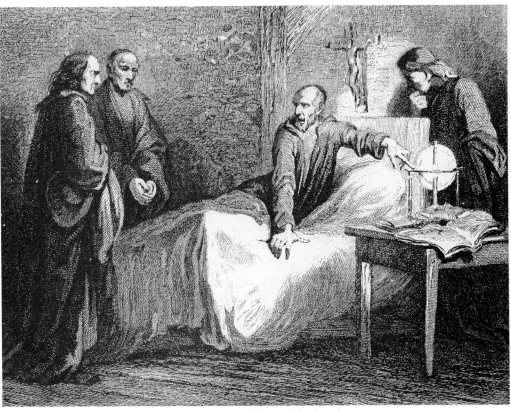

'I leave you the world!' St Ignatius on his deathbed, with his disciples

Whit Monday. All through a hot summer he lay in torment. When the beautiful Spanish autumn came, he was on the mend and decidedly bored at having to stay so long in bed. But it was the only way for the mutilated leg to set. Out of his restlessness and boredom came a desire for distractions of some kind and in turn was to lead to his surprising discovery.

Lying now in his family house in the village of Loyola, he wanted to while away the hours by feeding his fantasy life with the popular love stories of those days, and he asked for some of the silly tales of high romance that were in vogue at the court. But the village of his home was not the court and nothing of that kind could be found. His family could only provide him with books on the saints and about Christ. Out of sheer boredom he took them up and played with the fantasies they provoked in him. He gradually evolved a habit of passing the time through two kinds of fantasy; he would give space to imagining the life of the court and his romantic-cum-sexual possibilities there, and then with equal intensity he would enter into a daydream of becoming like the saints (as in these religious books). Boredom was banished for the moment, as these various images unfolded within him. Inigo had discovered in himself a great capacity for interior cinema and he ran the two films again and again, with many variations, through those late months of 1521.

But he was on the point of a greater discovery than how to beat bedridden boredom. He recounts later how 'one day it dawned on him' that there was 'a difference in his two subjects for thought'. Both of these gave him equal absorption and pleasure at the time, but when he set his imaginings aside a crucial difference of response emerged. Only in the aftermath of his fantasy periods, could he come to realise that the courtly images left him feeling empty and dissatisfied in himself, whereas with the religious images 'the joy remained unabated even when he stopped thinking of them'. Let him speak for himself in words from his third-person autobiography that sound remarkably modern:

> When he noticed the difference... he began to wonder at it. He understood from experience that one subject of thought left him dejection, while the other left him joy. This was his first ever insight into things of a spiritual kind. And later on, when he had gone through spiritual exercises, this experience was the starting-point for teaching his followers how to discern between one spirit and another.

For Ignatius, 'surface living' is not really satisfying. If we are to apply his insight to our own lives, it means paying attention to our deeper selves so that we can live – and die, without feeling cheated. Without feeling that we have missed opportunities, without feeling that we have not really lived. However, this is the choice we must make. It is a choice between a conscious decision to live life at a certain level or a more unconscious 'drifting through life'. The decision to live more fully is the first step towards faith, for ultimately 'Faith is man fully alive'.

Conclusion

> We have seen that science and technology have not been the answers to the deepest needs. There is evidence of this in the turn to fundamentalism, cults and the New Age Movement. There is evidence too that people are examining their own lives in order to find more meaning and that in doing so they are faced with a choice – to drift or to live more deliberately. This is our choice too.

Features of the Modern World	Effects/Responses
1. Scientific Revolution	a. early clash between science and religion
	b. This was caused by – biblical fundamentalism – science's claim to absolute truth
	c. More recently, there has been – recognition of the Bible as a book of religious truth – science seen as not the only form of truth – science raises greater questions of mystery
2. Technological Revolution	a. great technological advancement yet world problems not solved
	b. technology creates problems
	c. no technical solution – human solution – change behaviour
3. The search for meaning	a. fundamentalism
	b. cults
	c. New Age Movement
	d. first step towards faith

Revision exercises

1. List the positive and the negative effects of both science and religion.
2. Comment on the relationship between science and religion.
3. Write an essay on 'The possibility of faith in the modern world'.

The Growth of Faith

Chapter 5 builds on chapter 4 which talks about the need felt by many people in today's world to find fulfilment and meaning in their lives. Ultimately this is a call to live life more deeply. This is basic or human faith. Chapter 5 suggests that religious faith builds on human faith giving it an ultimate or eternal dimension. This ultimate or eternal dimension is experienced in the discovery of a sense of mystery in life which recognises that 'the world is charged with the grandeur of God'. However, to say that God is present in our experience of life is to make a decision about faith. We may choose not to recognise God in the world. Each decision has implications and the decision of faith makes demands on our lives.

Faith goes through different stages just as the human person does.

From human faith to religious faith to Christian faith

1. Human faith

At the beginning of his book *Stages of Faith,* the American psychologist James Fowler writes about an insight he had while driving to Asheville in North Carolina to give a seminar on faith. He had prepared a set of questions to ask his students when the thought struck him – how would he answer his own questions? The questions included:

a. What commands and receives your best time, your best energy?

b. What causes, dreams, goals or institutions are you pouring out your life for?

c. As you live your life, what power or powers do you fear or dread? What power or powers do you rely on or trust?

  To what or to whom are you committed in life? In death?

    d. With whom or with what group do you share your most sacred and
       private hopes for your life and for the lives of those you love?
    e. What are those most sacred hopes, those most compelling goals and
       purposes in your life?

Questions and exercises
1. Answer each of Fowler's questions for yourself.
2. Read your answers. What do you discover about yourself and
   your priorities?

Having spent forty minutes trying to answer these questions for himself, Fowler concluded that these are questions of faith. They are questions of faith because they help us identify the causes, the people and the events that make life meaningful for us. In this sense then, every human being is a person of faith since everyone needs to have meaning in his/her life. This is the mark of being human in that, as far as we know, none of the other creatures of the earth ask what life is about or search for meaning to give sense to the things that they do.

> We do not live by bread alone, sex alone, success alone, and certainly not by instinct alone. We require meaning.

If we dig a little deeper we discover what are called 'god values' in our lives. These 'god values' are the things that concern us ultimately. Examples of that 'ultimate concern' include things that centre on our own ego – work, prestige, recognition, power, influence, wealth. Our ultimate concern may be family, nation, Church, or even another person. Essentially it is that which is most important in our lives, that to which we give most time and attention.

2. Religious faith

There is nothing specifically religious about the understanding of faith that Fowler puts forward here. Rather, what he is talking about is human faith or basic faith, that which is concerned with what we value most as human beings. We may or may not choose to include things of a religious nature in the things that concern us most deeply. In chapter 3 we considered how people's thoughts, feelings and actions can lead them towards the idea of a transcendent, a God, but ultimately it is a decision that each person makes to recognise and acknowledge the presence of God in the midst of life. We see such a decision in the testimony of N.W. Clerk.

> In any case, marriage did one thing for me. I can no longer believe that religion comes from our subconscious wishful thinking and is only a sublimation of sex. In our years together, H. and I enjoyed love as a festival, in all possible ways, solemnly

and happily, romantically and realistically, sometimes as dramatic as a storm, sometimes as comfortable as a pair of slippers. We were contented fully, in heart and head and life. If God was only a substitute for love, we would have lost all interest in him. Why should we have cared for a substitute when we had the thing itself? But it was not that way. We both knew that we needed something beyond the other, something totally different. You might as well say that if two people are in love they have no need of reading, eating or breathing.

This acknowledgement of a religious divine element in life is not a suggestion that human faith and human concerns are not religious. Indeed the problem in the past and for many people still is that religious faith is divorced from human faith. The tragic result is that religion has become separated from life and is perceived as being either 'other worldly' or irrelevant to the basic human condition. What we are suggesting instead is that religious faith is born out of and builds on human faith. Religious faith gives an ultimate or eternal dimension to human faith. We remember Gabriel Marcel and his declaration that to profess love for another person is to say 'Thou, at least, shalt not die'. We see the need for the religious concern within the human concern. It is the hope that love overcomes even death. St Augustine's description of human restlessness only being filled by faith in God is another example of human need seeking divine fulfilment. To put this another way, we can say that most of our life centres around what are called ordinary experiences – the comings and goings of daily life. However, as Fr Dermot Lane puts it, 'there are those special moments when we go below the surface of life to discover a deeper dimension ...'

> This 'depth dimension' in life is the point where we discover such diverse realities as truth, meaning, value and beauty. (*The Experience of God*)

Such moments awaken in us a sense of the transcendent, a sense of mystery.

The discovery of mystery

Faith is the capacity to wonder. It is the readiness for surprise. It is the ability to share in a secret without understanding fully.

When the Russians launched the first Sputnik into space, the Soviet President, Nikita Krushchev, boasted that the astronauts had found no God – they had looked through the heavens but nowhere was he to be found. Contrast such an experience with that of Jim Irwin on the moon.

> The first time we could see the whole earth, we saw it as a ball in the sky. It was about the size of a basketball, and the most beautiful thing you could ever want to see in all your life. Then, as we got farther and farther away, it diminished in size. We saw it shrink to the size of a baseball, and then to the size of a golfball, and finally to the size of a marble, the most beautiful marble you can imagine. The earth is uncommonly lovely. It is the only warm object that we saw on our flight to the moon.........

Jim Irwin takes his first steps on the moon (NASA/Science Photo Library)

During this sort of flight, you are too busy to reflect on the splendour of space or on the secret awakenings that come from the inner flight that takes place at the same time. You have to try to register these experiences and examine them later. It has been sort of a slowbreaking revelation for me. The ultimate effect has been to deepen and strengthen all the religious insight I ever had. It has remade my faith. I had become a sceptic about getting guidance from God, and I know I had lost the feeling of his nearness. On the moon the total picture of the power of God and his Son Jesus Christ became abundantly clear to me.

'I felt an overwhelming sense of the presence of God on the moon. I felt his spirit more closely than I had ever felt it on the earth, right there beside me – it was amazing.'

To Rule the Night

Consider too the following poem, written by a Simon Community worker in Limerick.

I have seen a mother at a crib – and I know what love is.
I have gazed into the eyes of a child, and I know what faith is.
I have heard the pounding of the sea, and I know what power is.
I have seen a rainbow in the sky, and I know what beauty is.
I have planted a tree, and I know what hope is.
I have heard a wild bird sing – and I know what freedom is.
I have seen a chrysalis burst into life – and I know what mystery is.
I have lost my parents – I know what sadness is.
I have been in prison – I know what loneliness is.
I have lived with the destitute and I know what want is.

I have sat with the dying, and I know what fear is.
I have gazed into the sky alight with stars at night and I know what the Infinite is.
I have seen and felt all these things, so now I know who God is.

Questions and exercises
1. Who do you find more convincing, Nikita Krushchev or Jim Irwin?
2. Where do people find God?
3. Write your own poem entitled,
'I have seen ...... and I know what .... is.'

'The world is penetrated and filled with God's grace'.

This statement by the German theologian Karl Rahner summarises what Jim Irwin and the Simon Community worker recognise – namely that God is present in our daily experience of life and of the world if only we have eyes to see. Hence the experience of gazing into the eyes of a child, planting a tree and watching a mother at a crib become moments of faith, hope and love. This is illustrated in the human experience of being in love, as described in Pádraig Daly's poem 'Affair'.

92

You give my days importance:

Away from you ·
The lighting sea,
The calling of songbirds
The sheep moving down cliff-faces,
MEAN THEMSELVES ONLY.

You were everywhere I looked on the shore,
and at your going, I am inheritor of deserts.

With the eyes of love, places and experiences are loaded with meaning. Nothing means itself only. Everything becomes a link with and a memory of the beloved.

With the eyes of faith 'the world is charged with the grandeur of God'.

Exercise
'Love gives us eyes'. Discuss.

For the person of faith, then, God is not present *alongside* the rest of his/her life as an 'added extra'. Rather, he is present in all of our experiences of living and dying. Karl Rahner puts it like this:

> When someone experiences laughter or tears, bears responsibility, stands by the truth, breaks through the egoism of his life with other people, where someone hopes against hope, faces the shallowness and stupidity of the daily rush and bustle with humour and patience, refusing to become embittered; where someone learns to be silent and in this inner silence lets the evil in his heart die rather than spread outwards: in a word, wherever someone lives as he would like to live, combating his own egoism and the continual temptation to inner despair – there is the event of grace.
> *The Tablet,* 6 March 1971

Ultimately then, faith is the capacity to see the transcendent in life. It is born out of our religious or depth experience which, as Fr Dermot Lane writes:

> enables us to see that which was already there in our experience but which we failed to acknowledge explicitly in the first place.
> *The Experience of God*

To say that God is present in our experience of life is to make a decision about faith. In *Free to Believe,* Michael Paul Gallagher acknowledges that it is possible for atheists to share much of the journey that believers make in their search for freedom and meaning. There comes a time, however, when the choice must be made to take one road or the other – the way of belief or the way of non-belief. One cannot travel both, as the poet Robert Frost says in his poem, 'The Road not Taken'.

> *Two roads diverged in a yellow wood,*
> *And sorry I could not travel both*
> *And be one traveller, long I stood*
> *And looked down one as far as I could*
> *To where it bent in the undergrowth;*
>
> *Then took the other, as just as fair,*
> *and having perhaps the better claim,*
> *Because it was grassy and wanted wear;*
> *though as for that the passing there*
> *Had worn them really about the same,*
>
> *And both that morning equally lay*
> *In leaves no step had trodden black.*
> *Oh! I kept the first for another day!*
> *Yet knowing how way leads on to way,*
> *I doubted if I should ever come back.*
>
> *I shall be telling this with a sigh*
> *Somewhere ages and ages hence:*
> *Two roads diverged in a wood, and I –*
> *I took the one less travelled by,*
> *And that made all the difference.*

'One road or the other' – such is the decision one makes to see or not to see the religious dimension in life. We may glimpse such a dimension in life, ignore it, be indifferent to it or not see it at all. These are all possibilities as poet, Brendan Kennelly, and Jesuit, Gerard Hughes, point out.

Moments When the Light

There are moments when the light
Makes me start up, fright
In my heart as if I feared to see
Unbearable clarity about me.
Once, on Portobello Bridge,
I had the sudden privilege
Of seeing light leap from the sky
About five o'clock on an autumn day,
Defining every visible thing.
Unseen by one among the moving throng;
Road, bridge, factory, canal,
Stained swans and filthy reeds, all
The set homegoing faces
Filling motorcars and buses;
Then I knew that energy is but
Unconsciousness; if moving men could
See where they are going, they would
Stop and contemplate the light
And never move again until
They understood why it should spill
A sudden benediction on
The head of every homegoing man.
But no-one looked or saw the way
The waters danced for the visiting light
Or how green foliage glittered. It
Was ignored completely.
I knew the world is most at ease
With acceptable insanities,
Important nothings that command
The heart and mind of busy men
Who, had they seen it, might have praised
The light on Portobello Bridge.
But then, light broke. I looked. An evening glow.
Men go home because they do not know.

Brendan Kennelly

Question
Are there moments which make you 'start up' like the poet? Describe them.

In his book *God of Surprises,* Gerard Hughes tells the story of Jock, a tall, sandy-haired Scot.

> By trade he was an interior decorator, but unemployed. I was staying with friends who were having a room decorated and Jock was helping for the day. He worked like a monk with a vow of silence, his conversation limited to an occasional 'Aye' or 'Mmm'. Before joining us for a meal, he went off for a pint or two and then had wine at the meal, but he still remained locked in his inner cell, adding only an occasional 'Ta' to the 'Ayes' and 'Mmms'. Towards the end of the meal we began talking about North Wales, where I was then working. Jock looked up from his plate with obvious interest, then he began to speak.
>
> 'Aye,' he said, 'Ah wis in Wales in the summer, ma first holiday away from home'. I cannot now remember the details, for it was a long story. Either he had just been jilted by his girl friend and was trying to find her in North Wales, or he was trying to get away to forget her, but he continued, 'D'ye know whit ah found masel' doin? Walkin' the bloody moors wi' a wee dug. Ma mates wid've thought ah wis crazy, but ah felt happy. Ah came tae cliffs by the sea and just sat there. The sea looked affie big and ah felt very wee, but ah wis happy. Daft, isn't it? Ah cannie tell ma mates, 'cos they'd think ah wis kinky'.

It can be difficult to admit to the deeper and more sensitive side of our nature. It seems more acceptable to live out of what psychologists call the left-hand side of our brain – the rational-scientific and logical side. In a scientific, technological and material world where such thinking is encouraged and valued, it is easy to fear rejection. The right-hand side of the brain which is the source of wonder, imagination and feelings, is sometimes seen as weak, unproductive and soft. Yet, as we heard earlier from Pascal, 'the heart has its reasons of which reason knows nothing'. Deep down we are probably all aware of this but choose to mask it. As the American philosophy professor Dick Westley writes:

> At our center, we all share the human condition and are painfully the same no matter what the other differences between us. We cope with finitude, failure, advancing age, approaching death, and in the process come to recognize ourselves as broken and wounded. We mask that fact most of our waking hours, but when we cannot sleep and are alone in the still of night, we have an irresistible urge to tear off our masks and reveal our true selves to someone – to anyone – in the hope that he or she too will unmask and affirm the solidarity in weakness we all experience.
>
> *Redemptive Intimacy*

Questions
1. Have you ever felt like Jock? Explain.
2. Why can it be difficult to admit to the deeper and more sensitive side of our nature?
2. Should we admit to this side of our nature? If we did, what difference might it make to our priorities, to our relationships and to our lives?

3. The decision for Christian faith

Christian faith is impossible without some admission of the human weakness and limitation that Dick Westley writes about. It is impossible because the story of Jesus Christ is based on humankind's need of a saviour, of a redeemer. Christian faith is the acknowledgement that people are not their own saviours – that neither science nor technology, neither capitalism nor Marxism contain the recipe for human happiness. Christian faith is the recognition that Christ – the human face of God – is the ultimate author of human happiness, because through him death was conquered. This is the essence of Christian faith which each of us chooses to accept or reject.

> Either this man was the human face of God or else millions had based their lives on an illusion. My unbelieving friends might not accept that stark either-true-or-false. They might regard the historical figure of Jesus as a great religious leader, a spiritual genius, someone who embodies the hopes of humanity to live with love. They might see his story as a poem of visionary inspiration. They might reverence his life and death as they would that of Gandhi or Martin Luther King. But without crossing the threshhold into faith, they cannot reach what is central to the vision of Jesus in the Gospels – a relationship with God as his Father and a conviction that he came to inaugurate a new way of living called the Kingdom
>
> *Free to Believe,* Michael Paul Gallagher

In practice most of us maintain what might be called the 'threshold stance'. This is the more positive face of indifference where we do not reject the reality of Jesus, but neither do we take that step towards full faith in Jesus Christ because of the demands it might make on our lives. 'The new way of living' that Jesus called for can seem too demanding of our cosy situation. It is easier to drift along, 'to reverence from afar'.

Questions
1. Have millions of Christians based their lives on an illusion?
2. Why is it difficult to choose to be a Christian?
3. The first Christians were called 'followers of the Way'. Why?

The decision for faith has two dimensions to it. Firstly, it asks us to take a risk – to surrender to the greater reality we call God. This concept may be difficult to understand until we consider what is involved in loving another person. Ultimately we have to take a risk. We have to trust, to open ourselves up to another person, to hazard being vulnerable. We may end up being hurt but that is the risk we have got to take if we ever wish to love. Faith, then, is the willingness to believe without having all the evidence. It is the willingness to trust because we have a sense that it is right.

Secondly, Christian faith demands a practical response from us.

> What does it profit, my brethren, if a man says he has faith but not works? Can his faith save him? If a brother or sister is ill-clad or in lack of daily food, and one of us says to them, 'Go in peace, be warmed and filled,' without giving them the things needed for the body, what does it profit? So faith by itself, if it has no works, is dead (James 2:14-17).

Stages of faith

At the age of four, I knew that God was everywhere. I spoke to him, and sometimes he listened with sympathy. It was an unforgettable occasion in boyhood when he did indeed send me a bicycle.

As I grew towards manhood, the more I learned, the less I believed in God. I told myself that he had been invented by ancients who feared the eternal darkness of death. Even worse, they had fashioned him into their likeness.

When I was twenty-one my superior intellect told me that God was a fake.

Then one day I felt a new experience. I saw the miracle of birth, and it turned my wandering mind around. I had seen babies before, of course, in prams, had cooed at them, chucked them under the chin, observed their gummy grins and hoped they would not cry.

But this miracle was Virginia Lee, a child of my own. She was just another infant (an exceptionally beautiful one, to be sure), but so close to me that this time I questioned the birth and life.

She was the result of the fusion of two bodies in love, but how did an ovum learn to roll to the womb? What caused spermatozoa to fertilise an egg? And what far off deity told that ovum to split and split to form a foetus, to devise its own chemical factory and absorb nourishment from its mother?

How I wondered, could an infant, unconscious of life and the struggle for existence, fashion the correct number of limbs and toes and fingers and eyes and ears? Did all that do itself?

If it was a matter of genes, did they fashion themselves? Maybe they evolved over millions of years. From what? I began to doubt my doubts. (Jim Bishop – on the birth of his daughter)
Mystery of God, Teacher's Book

The decision for faith is not a once-off single commitment. Rather, as James Fowler points out, there are stages of faith that are linked with the stages of human development and one's experiences of life. The faith of the adult is very different from that of the child. St Paul puts it like this:

> When I was a child, I spoke like a child,
> I thought like a child, I reasoned like a child,
> When I became a man, I gave up childish ways.
> (1 Cor 13:11)

The problem for many of us, however, is that our images of God are those we acquired in childhood. These images of God seem childish and immature to us when we reach adulthood. However, instead of replacing such childish images and concepts with more adult ones as we do in other areas of life, we abandon faith altogether. We develop adult thinking about ourselves and our world but all too often we remain immature in our faith, a situation that makes faith seem naive and simple, or we abandon such faith because it does not do justice to our adult experience of life and the intelligent world. Either way we are not doing justice to the experience of faith. To abandon one's faith because one has come to a reasoned and well-informed decision about the existence of God, is one thing. To abandon one's faith because one has never developed an adult understanding of what it means to believe is unworthy of one's intelligence and the phenomenon of faith. An adult, informed understanding of the nature of faith is thus necessary if we are to make a mature decision about faith. This is because, as we have said already, faith develops in stages that roughly match human development.

Summary of James Fowler, STAGES OF FAITH:

Pre-stage: primal faith rooted in basic trust (infancy)

Stage I (age 2-6: intuitive, undifferentiated IMAGES (protection, threat, etc.)

Stage II (age 6-12): meaning through STORIES and the ability to enter perspective of others

Stage III (age 13-19): emerging identity through RELATIONSHIPS and emotional solidarity with others. Faith: unreflective, pre-decision synthesis – often inarticulate

Stage IV (age 20-30+): after becoming distanced from convention, can find new responsibility for CHOICES; faith of explicit conviction and commitment; able to swim against the tide; hence critical, alert believer

Stage V (age 35+): Mid-life collapse of clarities; enter into darker complexity: new capacity to cope with AMBIGUITY, deeper spiritual life, ready to serve justice

Stage (Age 50+): More universal serenity: FREEDOM for steady self-transcendence, open to goodness in everything, sense of unity with God

Questions and exercises
1. Draw a time-chart of your life to date and
   a. state the priority of each stage of your life;
   b. describe the role of religion at each stage.
2. What is the danger of holding on to childhood images of God?
3. Explain in your own words what prompted Jim Bishop to re-examine his understanding of God.

Faith and doubt

If we think about the bigger decisions that we make in life, we find that they are usually preceded or accompanied by the experience of doubt. In such situations 'doubt arises from the incompleteness of human evidence or the lack of personal security in the choices we make'.

The obvious example of such an experience of doubt is the decision to marry where, in the last analysis, we take a risk. Faith, which can be compared more to trust between people than to scientific certainty, may also be accompanied by the experience of doubt. In so far as personal faith is a relationship between ourselves and God the kind of doubt present in all relationships may be present in this faith relationship. Indeed, in so far as we are human and lack complete knowledge of the God we believe in, the experience of doubt seems very natural. The cry of the man who said to Christ 'I believe, help my unbelief' rings true in the heart of many a believer. In yet another book on faith, *Help my Unbelief,* Michael Paul Gallagher describes his experience of saying Mass as an atheist.

> It was a Thursday evening at Mass that I entered into my atheism in a deeper way than ever before. That may sound like the opening sentence of a first-person novel, but in fact it is true of the author of this book. Does that seem shocking? I believe it to be a not uncommon reality, even for religious people, that they run into bouts of temporary atheism and I want to open this discussion by describing one of mine. A short experience, yes, but one that proved more revealing than other more lingering eclipses of faith.

> The context may have had something to do with it – it often does. I had a short night's sleep and a longish and somewhat unsatisfactory day. The actual trigger for atheism came, paradoxically, with the reading of the Gospel at Mass. It was about the Sadducees disputing with Christ over resurrection from the dead, and, with a little form-criticism in my head, I found myself disbelieving that these words were ever spoken by Jesus; they were surely put into his mouth by some controversy in the early Church. How much was added? The question soon became magnified into 'How much was fabricated?' From that inner standpoint I stayed unusually alert to the words of the Mass, but in a deeply doubting vein. I found myself, as it were, watching from the outside, and hearing words with a certain nostalgia for their meaning, almost as if I

had been an atheist for years and was now revisiting a familiar scene of worship. In one sense I struggled with the thoughts and movements of spirit, but it remained an alarming and lonely experience to be there with my community, and yet to feel cut off from the core of why we are gathered there. For the others it was just an ordinary evening Mass, low-key and undemonstrative. For me it was suddenly dramatic. I wondered if I would ever emerge from this state of finding it incredible. Concelebrating, I found the words of the consecration painful in a strange way, hoping that they could be true but sensing that they were not. Through the post-consecration prayers I joined in the words, wishing that the living and the dead could be blessed, but fearing that it was all a sham, a façade on human fears.

The whole liturgy seemed a rich symbolic wisdom with only imaginary foundations: it was what mankind had built around the story of Jesus. Sharing the sign of peace with others was an experience of sadness: we thought we were giving one another something from God but we might have only one another, alone in the world. More intense still was the moment of holding the host prior to communion, because it was a stark either-or; true or false, with no middle ground. Either this bread was the presence of Jesus or the whole thing was fantasy. Either the Resurrection was an event, or the whole edifice of our religion was a grotesque exaggeration of one preacher's life in Palestine.

After receiving communion I found myself praying, or trying to pray, using the famous words from the father of the possessed boy in the gospels: 'Lord, I believe, but help my unbelief' (Mark 9:24). I simply repeated them inside myself. Nothing much happened and yet something changed. Perhaps I can best express it by borrowing two utterly simple words from the end of George Herbert's sonnet on prayer when, after listing phrase after phrase for the range of the experience of prayer, he concludes that it means 'something understood'.

What did I understand or begin to understand after communion and at close of my Mass in atheistic mood? I understood that faith was a more extraordinary gift than I had ever realised. I glimpsed the potential doubt that can never be separated from faith in this life. Most of all I came to see, yet again, that faith is something quite different from the mere accuracy of objective truth.

We are human, and just as there is the element of doubt in all our relationships, so too there is the element of doubt in faith. So we choose to believe in God, mindful that we will never find the kind of certainty longed for by Woody Allen:

I am plagued by doubts. What if everything is an illusion and nothing exists? In that case I definitely overpaid for the carpet. If only God would give me some clear sign; like making a large deposit in my name at a Swiss bank.

We choose to believe, mindful that doubt exists for the unbeliever too. Cardinal Ratzinger uses a Jewish story told by Martin Buber to make this point.

A believer in the Enlightenment, a very learned man who emphasised reason as the only source of truth, visited the Rabbi of Barditchev to argue with him and shatter what he considered his old-fashioned proofs of his faith. When he arrived, the Rabbi ignored him, and kept walking up and down the room with a book in his hand. Then suddenly he looked at the learned man and said 'But perhaps it is true after all.' The learned man was taken aback. Then the Rabbi turned to him and said. 'The great scholars of the Torah (Bible) with whom you have argued wasted their words on you; as you departed you laughed at them. They were unable to lay God and his kingdom on the table before you, and nor can I. But think, my son, *perhaps it is true.*' The learned man opposed him but his terrible 'Perhaps' lingered with him and finally broke his resistance.

Thus, both the believer and the unbeliever share, each in his own way, doubt *and* belief, if they do not hide away from themselves and from the truth of their being.
Introduction to Christianity

Questions
1. What things in your life are you least certain about?
2. What doubts do you have about faith?
3. In the midst of his experience of doubt Fr Michael Paul Gallagher realised that faith was an 'extraordinary gift'. What do you think he meant by this?
4. What does it mean to say that the unbeliever doubts too?

SUMMARY CHART

Type of Faith	Description
1. Human Faith	concerns the causes, the people and the events that make life meaningful for us, e.g. work, power, influence, wealth, family, nation, friends etc.
2. Religious Faith	a. is aware of a sense of mystery in life. b. recognises and acknowledges the presence of God in the midst of life: 'The world is charged with the grandeur of God.' c. decides for the way of belief as the way of making sense of one's life and one's world.
3. Christian Faith	a. is the recognition that Christ – the human face of God – is the ultimate author of human happiness. b. goes through stages as we mature and age. c. includes doubt.

CHAPTER 6

The Phenomenon of Religion

This chapter considers the nature and the purpose of religion. It acknowledges that the experiences of joy and happiness, of suffering and death, the question of how life should be lived, are the concerns of human beings wherever and whenever they live. Vatican II outlined three main questions which religion addresses:

1. the meaning of life
2. the mystery of existence
3. how we should love

There are characteristic elements that can be identified in many religions: Ritual, Mythology, Doctrine, Ethics, Institution, Experiential/Spiritual dimension.

Introduction

Earlier we looked at the question of **Faith**. We considered why people believe and why they do not believe. We considered the possibility of faith in the modern world; in particular, we focused on the search that goes on in the human heart to find meaning and to live authentically. In this context then, our emphasis was on the **individual** and the personal decision to accept or not to accept faith as a way of making sense of our life and our world.

In this section, we move beyond the individual search as such. We move into the realms of history and geography which remind us that our western way of life in the twentieth century, our attitudes and beliefs, are not the only ones. We are but a dot in the whole history of the universe. Yet the work of archaeologists, historians and geographers shows us that there can be a remarkable similarity between the concerns of people living in ancient Egypt (5,000 BC) and people living in western Europe in this century. THE EXPERIENCES OF JOY AND HAPPINESS, OF SUFFERING AND DEATH, THE QUESTION OF HOW LIFE SHOULD BE LIVED, ARE THE CONCERNS OF HUMAN BEINGS, WHEREVER AND WHENEVER THEY LIVE.

Religion and the History of Humankind

Religion is a universal phenomenon. It extends right back in history to the beginning of human activity. Traces of what we might term religious activity have been found amongst people in every part of the world. Religion has been part of the development of the great civilisations of the world. It is impossible to study the history of our ancestors without becoming aware of their religious beliefs, language and rituals. We know that the peoples of ancient Greece and Rome believed in many gods. We know that the ancient Egyptians buried their dead in such a way as to suggest belief in an afterlife. We know that the Druids of pre-Christian Ireland led the people in acts of public worship.

Religion has also served as a vehicle for expressing some of the deepest human experiences – wonder and mystery, sorrow and loss, great joy.

Questions
1. Why do you think people turn to religion?
2. Why have religions survived through the ages?

The Nature of Religion

The universality and significance of religion in human history prompts us to ask: What is religion, what purpose does religion serve? Vatican II, in its document on the relation of the Catholic Church to non-Christian religions (*Declaration on Non-Christian Religions*), identified three main characteristics of religion.

1. People look to their different religions for an answer to the unsolved riddles of human existence. The problems that weigh heavily on people's hearts are the same today as in ages past.

The Council then went on to list some of the questions and concerns of human beings.

What is the human person? What is the meaning of and purpose of life? What is upright behaviour and what is sinful? Where does suffering originate, and what end does it serve? How can genuine happiness be found? What happens at death? What is judgment? What rewards follow death? And, finally, what is the ultimate mystery beyond human explanation, which embraces our entire universe, from which we take our origin and towards which we tend?
(Par. 1)

These are questions about the meaning and purpose of life. It is when people come up with common answers to such questions that religion is born. In this way religion gives answers and meaning to the deeper questions about life. We shall see this more clearly when we look at the religions of our earliest ancestors and at the main world religions today.

Exercise or group work
Consider the questions posed by Vatican II
1. What answer would you give to each of these questions?
2. How do your answers compare with those of other students in your class?

2. Religion is a response to the experience of mystery – to revelation.

It would be a mistake to think that religion is only about providing answers and giving meaning to life. If this were the case, then it could be said that people invent religion to provide meaning and comfort for themselves. This was what Karl Marx had in mind when he called religion the 'opium of the people'. Vatican II recognised this when it pointed out a second characteristic of religion.

> Throughout history, even to the present day, there is found among different peoples a certain awareness of a *hidden power*, which lies behind the course of nature and the events of human life. At times there is present even a recognition of a supreme being, or still more of a father (*Declaration on Non-Christian Religions*, 2)

There are moments in all our lives – moments when we experience beauty, love, tenderness – when we glimpse something mysterious, a hidden power or presence which is not of our own making. If we are sensitive to such a moment we feel uplifted, generous, at peace with ourselves and our world. When we reflect on such experience, we discover something of the truth of ourselves and the world. Perhaps it would be more correct to say that something of the truth of ourselves and our world is revealed to us in such an experience. This insight is a moment of revelation for us.

Of course it is possible to miss such a moment of revelation or to dismiss it as a foolish daydream. It is possible also to appreciate that moment for what it was and then forget about it as we get on with our daily lives. Or we may decide that such moments are special experiences that put us in touch with what is most deep and most true about life – something mysterious, something great, something other. In this sense such moments can be described as religious. Albert Einstein put it like this:

> The most beautiful experience we can have is the mysterious.... whoever does not know it and can no longer wonder, no longer marvel, is as good as dead, and his eyes are dimmed.... it is this knowledge and this emotion that constitute true religiosity; in this sense and in this alone, I am a deeply religious man.

This recognition of the mysterious element in life, this 'awareness of a hidden power which lies behind the course of nature and the events of human life' is the second characteristic of primitive and world religions. When people pray or worship they are responding to the presence they have experienced. In a real sense then, true religion cannot be forced on people. It only makes sense if they have become aware of this mysterious presence. Then their religion is their way of responding to this presence.

Exercise
Reflect on moments when you have experienced beauty, love or tenderness in your own life. How did you feel at such moments?

3. Religion influences our way of life

The third characteristic of religion builds on the second. 'This awareness and recognition results in a way of life that is imbued with a deep religious sense' (*Declaration on Non-Christian Religions*, 2).

What Vatican II is saying here is that our awareness of a power beyond ourselves influences our way of life. When someone has such an awareness certain things follow which may not make sense to a person who has never recognised this greater power. Perhaps the best example to show what we mean here is the experience of being in love. When two people are in love, everything they feel and do is influenced by the experience of being in love. Even ordinary, everyday things take on a new meaning because they are done with or for the beloved. The thoughts and action of such a couple may or may not make sense to those outside the relationship or to those who have never had the experience of being in love. Things make sense to such a couple because they are done in the context of love. To paraphrase Vatican II – their way of life is imbued with a sense of love.

Applying this example to the question of religion and life, we can say that when a person believes, when a person has a religious sense, then that person's way of life is influenced and affected by this belief. Without this religious sense, then aspects of a way of life such as worship, or certain moral beliefs and actions, may be seen as either not making sense or as being imposed.

Exercise
'People can live a perfectly good life without reference to religion'. Discuss.

The characteristics of religion

It is difficult to define religion. Some of the elements which go to make up what we call 'religion' may equally apply to ideologies like Communism and Fascism which, like religion, are used to explain the purpose of human life in history and point the way towards living such a life. Communism, for instance, proposes a classless society where everything is shared equally and the individual works for the good of the State. This becomes the purpose of the individual's life.

Many of those who have believed in ideologies like Communism or Fascism have devoted their lives to such beliefs with the same devotion as a follower of religion might. So we are left with the question: What is meant by religion and how does religion differ from ideology? The following six characteristics of religion have been identified:

1. RITUAL: Ritual can be understood as a way or a variety of ways of acting out beliefs. Every religion has its rituals – worship, preaching, prayers and so on, which help to express and give visible form to deeply-held beliefs which may be abstract. The role which ritual plays in religion goes right back to earliest times. The Great Bath at Mohenjo Daro in the Indus Valley, for example, is thought to have been associated with ancient ritual use – probably some kind of cleansing.

The Great Bath at Mohenjo Daro

Sacrificial rituals are part of many religions where offerings are made to the divine either as a form of thanksgiving or so that the divine will be pleased. The ancient Jewish tradition of the Temple before it was destroyed in 70 AD was preoccupied with rituals of sacrifice. Moreover, such ritual, for example the Passover Feast, does not merely commemorate a past event. Through entering into the elements of the ritual the people relive what happened at the first Passover Feast.

As time goes on, rituals may become very ordered and very formalised. One of the problems with this is that people may be unaware of the original intentions and beliefs which the ritual sought to express. Language undergoes change, actions may come to mean different things and so rituals which were highly meaningful and relevant in the past may seem empty and outdated to a more modern age.

? Exercise
Give an example of any ritual in which you have participated.
State its purpose and describe the rite involved.

2. MYTHOLOGY: This is the story side of religion. All faiths have handed down vital stories – some historical, some about mysterious questions like the origin of the world or the end of time, some about the founders, Moses, Buddha, Muhammad, some which are parables and stories about the actions of the gods. Some of these stories are rooted in history, others are not – they are myths. That is not to say that they are untrue. Rather, myths are stories which encapsulate a deep truth that is shared by a large group of people, who are bound together by a common faith. For example the stories of creation which we find at the beginning of the Book of Genesis and which are accepted by both Jews and Christians are myths which express the truth that God is Creator and seek to explain how evil, suffering and death came into the world. The stories, while they may not  be literally true, seek nonetheless to convey truths which are very profound. Our scientific western world has difficulty accepting what is not literally true. Myths fare better in traditions of the east where different ways of expressing truth are more readily accepted.

? Question and exercise
What does it mean to say that 'myths are stories which encapsulate a deep truth'?
Give an example of such a myth.

109

3. DOCTRINE: Doctrines are statements of religious belief or the content of faith. For example in Christianity the statement 'Jesus is both God and Man' is a doctrine or statement of what Christians believe. Doctrines aim to clarify what is believed so that faith can be preserved and handed on to other believers. Doctrines play a significant role in all major religions. It would be difficult, for example, to communicate what is important to Buddhists without being able to refer to some statement which contains the basis of their faith. Thus the Four Noble Truths of Buddhism, which state what Buddhists believe fundamentally, are an example of doctrine.

Doctrines, therefore, are the thought-out expression of what is believed. They are usually formulated or put together after the experience or event which inspired them. Thus the early Christian believers experienced Jesus before they made doctrinal statements about him, for example, 'Jesus is both God and man'.

Exercise
Outline some of the doctrines/statements of any movement or organisation with which you are familiar.

4. ETHICS: Moral or ethical codes tend to be part of most religions. They exist to describe the kind of behaviour which is acceptable in or desired by a follower of a particular religion. These moral or ethical codes tend to have two functions: (a) they describe which kind of behaviour best helps people live together in society. Thus murder and theft are condemned because they would deny other people's right to life and to property; (b) they list standards of practices of behaviour like self-control, fasting, abstaining from alcohol etc., as they are deemed to be important for spiritual development.

Many of the world religions contain similar moral codes. In Judaism the law or moral code contains the Ten Commandments. These are also accepted by Christians and are very similar to the commands contained in the Muslim Qur'an. All of these religions accept that murder, adultery, theft and giving false evidence are wrong. The Qur'an places a very strong emphasis on family relationships.

Hinduism and Buddhism teach the importance of *ahimsa* (non-violence) as well as truthfulness, honesty and chastity. The life of Mahatma Gandhi and the spectacle of Buddhist monks marching for nuclear disarmament are examples of the Buddhist commitment to *ahimsa*.

Islamic life has been particularly controlled by the law or *Shari'a* which shapes both the individual's life and society. The individual must pray daily, give alms to the poor etc. Islamic society must have certain institutions such as marriage, modes of banking etc.

Question
Why are religions concerned with ethics and morality? Should they be?

5. INSTITUTION: Religions tend to be organised. Traditionally to be a Hindu meant that one was part of a particular *caste*. The caste a person belonged to was both an indication of his or her social position as well as his or her level of religious purity.

The institution is therefore the concrete, visible form which religious belief takes. It is the group of people who profess a certain common faith. Ideally it seeks to remain true to the belief it professes, though at times its members may fail. The institution is important in so far as it shows that religion is a community affair. It is not simply the concern of the individual. Frequently the institution has a teaching role where doctrine and ethics are concerned. It also plays a key role in the rituals of a particular religion.

Questions
1. Why do people sometimes react negatively to institutions?
2. Are institutions necessary? Why/Why not?

6. EXPERIENTIAL OR SPIRITUAL DIMENSION: The five dimensions of religion described above are found in all the main religions and they show us the different aspects of religion. However, it could be argued that these five dimensions could also apply to ideologies such as Fascism and Communism. In Nazism, for instance, we see the following elements :

> RITUAL: uniforms, parades, the Nazi salute, the swastika
> MYTHOLOGY: belief in the superman theory based on the ideas of
> the German philosopher Nietzsche
> DOCTRINE: the State should have complete control over every aspect
> of people's lives, both public and private – the totalitarian State
> ETHICS: obedience to the leader – Der Führer
> INSTITUTION: the Nazi Party

It is the sixth dimension of religion – the *experiential* or *spiritual* dimension of religion which differentiates religion and ideology. This is what we call religious experience – an awareness of a sense of mystery or, as one writer called it, '*the idea of the holy*'. This is an awareness of some power greater than oneself. It inspired the visions of the Prophet Muhammad and the enlightenment of Buddha. In religious traditions prayer and meditation, spiritual exercises and yoga are used to enable people to experience the holy. However, such an experience is not seen as being an end in itself, rather, the experience leads people to commit themselves to a way of life that is in keeping with their experience of the holy.

SUMMARY CHART

1. The purposes of religion as identified by Vatican II	a. Religion is a source of meaning. b. Religion is a response to the experience of mystery. c. Religion influences our way of life.
2. The six characteristics of religion	a. Ritual b. Mythology c. Doctrine d. Ethics e. Institution f. Experiential/spiritual dimension

Revision questions and exercises
1. Outline the three purposes of religion.
2. Select one of the characteristics of religion as described above and apply it to any of the world religions with which you are familiar.
3. 'Religion and politics are really the same thing.'
   Discuss/Debate.

CHAPTER 7

Prehistoric Religion

This chapter investigates the archaeological evidence for prehistoric religious activity. (Much of this is already familiar to students who have studied Junior Certificate History.) For prehistoric people, religion had three roles:

1. It had to do with that which concerned people ultimately.
2. It had to do with coming to grips with death.
3. It had to do with an awareness of a sense of the sacred.

Introduction

In her book, *Great Religions of the World*, Loretta Pastva tells this story.

> A companion of the British zoologist Jane Goodall once described a chimpanzee that stood as if lost in contemplation before a deep waterfall in a tropical forest. The chimp moved closer to the waterfall and began to rock, giving a round of 'pant-hoot' calls. Becoming more and more excited, it ran back and forth, leaping in the air, calling louder, beating on trees with its fists and running back again to the stunning light.

> Unlike typical groups of chimps which do 'rain dances' when surprised by a sudden storm, this animal returned to the spot on other days as if drawn there for no other reason than to perform its ritual before the magnificent power of the falls. We might wonder, Is this chimp's behaviour similar to the way that the early ancestors of us *Homo sapiens* first responded to the wonders of the natural world?

We cannot answer this question with any degree of certainty. This is so because prehistoric people existed at a time before writing began. Therefore there are no written records, no descriptions or stories to tell us about how our earliest ancestors lived. However, as the study of history at Junior Certificate level showed us, we are not without some clues about the lives of the earliest human beings.

When studying the people of prehistoric times, historians rely on the work of archaeologists as well as the stories carried by word of mouth in the form of legends. By excavating sites, putting together the items found (such as pieces of pottery, human and animal bones, stone and metal tools, coins, remnants of food and even pollen grains), archaeologists, together with historians, are able to put together descriptions of how people lived in the past.

Archaeological evidence of 'religious' activity in prehistoric peoples

The earliest indications of 'religious' belief and practice are not found in written documents but in the remains of 100,000-year-old burial sites which have been excavated by archaeologists. Neanderthal people (called after the Neander Valley in Germany where the earliest evidence was found) used to bury their dead. In this very act we find something which distinguishes people from animals – animals leave their dead: people have always felt the need to bury their dead with care and dignity. Frequently, too, the dead were buried with ornaments, tools and even food, which may well testify to some form of belief in an afterlife. Sometimes layers of ashes were found near grave sites which suggest that memorial meals may have been held after the burials.

Ice Age double burial from the Grotte des Infants, near Menton, France

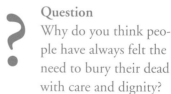

Question
Why do you think people have always felt the need to bury their dead with care and dignity?

Legend and early religion

Egyptian religion is the oldest religion of which we have documentary evidence. Once again, coming to grips with death is a main element of this religion. The Legend of Osiris, which seems to come from a time before 2,500 BC, indicates some belief in an afterlife.

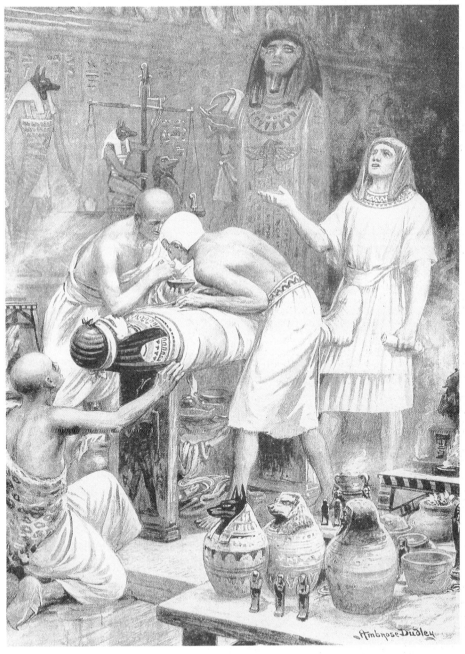

Mummification in Ancient Egypt

Osiris, according to the story, was a good and wise king who lived long ago in Egypt. He was hated by his brother, Set, who found the opportunity to murder Osiris and then threw his dismembered body into the Nile. Isis, the wife of Osiris, searched for her husband and, with the help of her sister and of the gods, she was able to find the body which was reconstituted and raised to life. Instead of returning to the land of the living, however, Osiris then became the god of the dead.

The Nature of Religion

This legend became the basis of the funeral ceremony which was carried out when someone died. While the dead person's body was being embalmed the story was recited with the intention that what happened to Osiris would also happen to the dead person. In other words, the dead person would come back to life. Sometimes the name 'Osiris' was added to the name of the dead person for the same purpose. The Pyramid texts which were used when a pharaoh died included the words, 'As you do not die, Osiris, so too this man does not die.'

? Question
What picture do we get of the role that religion played in the lives of ancient people?

1. Religion had to do with that which concerned people ultimately.

Hunting was the most important aspect of early human life as people were dependent on the hunt for their source of food – and food meant the difference between life and death. It is not surprising then that the hunt had huge religious significance for people, and became the subject-matter of their cave paintings, an example of which we see here.

This is the most famous of all cave paintings, '*The Dancing Sorcerer*', found at Ariège in France. The mixture of animal features on the costume may well be because of the close relationship that early societies had with the animals on which they depended for food and clothes.

These paintings have high artistic value but, as the scholar Ninian Smart points out, this was not their main purpose. Rather, their purpose held a magical element:

By drawing the animals successfully hunted they would in fact *be* successfully hunted.

Moreover these paintings took a long time to find as they were drawn in obscure parts and not in obvious places. This may suggest that they held some sacred significance for the people, though we can only guess at this. What is undisputed is the fact that the hunt played a crucial role in people's lives. It was a matter of life and death for them. If it was successful they ate – if not they starved.

The ancient Egyptian mother-goddess, Isis, with her son, Horus

Religion is about the 'ultimate concern', that which is most deeply important to people. It is therefore easy to see how the hunt held religious significance for prehistoric people. The *success of the hunt* was indeed a matter of ultimate concern for these people. Thus the earliest forms of religion may well have included prayers and rituals before the hunt. It may have included sacrifices of slain animals and prayers of thanksgiving and celebration after the hunt.

Later, with the beginning of farming, the *soil and its fertility* became the ultimate concern for people. So the religious focus moved from hunting scenes to fertility rites. Farming now became the ultimate concern of people who depended on the fruits of the soil and the flesh of farmed animals for survival. So fertility gods and associated rites and rituals became very important. A great deal of archaeological evidence suggests that a mother-goddess was very significant across Europe and Asia.

2. Religion had to do with coming to grips with death.

Early people believed in *panvitalism* – that is the idea that all things are alive. The world was seen as a womb-like source of life from which everything – nature, animals and humans – drew energy to live. They came from the life of the earth and when they died they went back into the life of that same earth. Death seemed very unreal within this understanding. 'If everything is alive, how can any animal or person really be dead?' This dilemma may well have led to the idea of some sort of survival after death. Again the archaeological evidence is crucial here. The excavation of burial sites has led archaeologists to conclude that prehistoric peoples practised some form of funeral rite. Three features of their burial customs are especially significant:

1. At a number of sites red ochre was sprinkled on the bodies. This powder probably symbolised blood and, therefore, life, as it does for Australian aboriginals today. The fact that it was used so often may suggest that these early people wanted to bring about life after death or at least hope for the continued life of those who had died.

2. Many bodies were buried surrounded by tools, ornaments and weapons, suggesting that the dead person would need such things when he came back to life. The burial practices of the Egyptians are perhaps the best examples of this: the Pharaohs were buried, together

with their worldly goods and their slain servants. Indeed, all Egyptians who could afford it had their bodies preserved or embalmed, suggesting that if the dead body were preserved, it would live again after death.

3. Some bodies were found in a sleeping position corresponding to that of a child in the womb. Perhaps this was in the hope that life would be continued through being born again into this world or another.

However we interpret this evidence, it is clear that death was a deep and mysterious experience for those people and that the earliest expressions of religion had a lot to do with coming to grips with death. Indeed, we can say that little has changed in this regard for human beings thousands of years later.

One other way that primitive religion dealt with death was through belief in *animism*. The Latin word *anima* means soul, life, spirit; thus animism is the belief that some kind of spiritual dimension exists within the bodies of animals and humans. This gave rise to the belief that even if bodies die, the anima, or soul, lives on.

Question
How do people today try to come to grips with death?

3. Religion has to do with an awareness of a sense of mystery or the sacred

It would be a mistake to conclude that early religious sense only developed out of a need to come to grips with death. We have already hinted at some awareness of the idea of a greater being or beings when we described the worship of spirits of animals and of fertility gods or goddesses. Worship follows upon an awareness of something greater than people, something that has to do with mystery or what we describe as 'sacred' or 'the holy'.

> If we asked our paleolithic or neolithic ancestors why they practised religious rituals in connection with hunting, death and fertility, they would hardly be inclined to answer in terms of our modern social sciences. They would not tell us that they were acting religiously for the purpose of survival or simply in order to confront the overwhelming threat of death.... Instead they would insist that they were responding to a 'presence'. Their religion, they would stipulate, is a *communion* with holy or sacred powers.
>
> *What is Religion?* J. F. Haught

If we look at the archaeological evidence we discover hints that early people were aware of greater powers and worshipped gods they believed had such powers. Some of the megalithic buildings that date back to the Stone Age may have been used as temples for worship. The huge stone monument at Stonehenge in southern Britain may well be an example of such a building. The people who built it may have thought that the sun and moon were gods. They built Stonehenge so that on Midsummer's Day, someone standing at the centre of the circle can see the sun rising over a particular stone.

CONCLUSION

In this chapter we considered the evidence that suggests that there was a religious sense in human beings from the earliest times. We discovered that religion for these people centred on three things:

1. Those things that concerned people ultimately
2. Coming to grips with death
3. Responding to the experience of mystery

Despite the extraordinary developments that have taken place since the Stone Age it is interesting to note that these are still the concerns of people in today's world.

SUMMARY CHART	
1. Evidence of prehistoric religion	a. Religion is a source of meaning.
	b. Religion is a response to the experience of mystery.
	c. Religion influences our way of life.
2. The role of religion in the lives of prehistoric people	a. Ritual
	b. Mythology
	c. Doctrine
	d. Ethics
	e. Institution
	f. Experiential/spiritual dimension

Revision questions and exercises

1. Look up your first-year history book or a library book to find out about the burial customs of prehistoric peoples and of ancient civilisations. What do you conclude about their attitudes to death from the evidence as it exists?
2. Do you think it is reasonable to conclude from the evidence that prehistoric peoples were 'religious'? Explain your answer.

CHAPTER 8

World Religions today

This chapter begins by explaining some of the terms we associate with world religions. It proceeds to consider three of the main world religions in terms of their beliefs and practices. These are Hinduism, Buddhism and Islam.

Introduction

The study of world religions is a complex task. It is complex because religion itself is complex. The language, the ideas and the symbols vary from religion to religion. Religion is part of culture and so, to understand a particular world religion, it is very often necessary to understand something of the culture in which it was born. Moreover, most religions would contend that people cannot come to truly know them without experiencing them at first hand. There is a distinct difference between 'knowing about' a religion and 'knowing' a religion in terms of experiencing its beliefs and practices.

An understanding of world religions is made even more difficult for someone living in Ireland as the majority of people living in this country belong to one or other of the Christian Churches. It is not often that we come to know someone of a faith other than Christianity. Our awareness of religions outside Christianity is often through stories or historical events.

This chapter will take a look at some of the main beliefs and practices of some of the main religions which have helped to shape our world.

Here is an explanation of some of the terms used:

1. World religions: religions which are practised by people in many different nations, who speak different languages and have different cultures and traditions. Thus, for example, we find Islam in Central America, Central Africa and the Middle East. A study of the map of world religions (p.122) shows the locations of the main world religions as practised throughout the world.

There are two main types of world religion:

> The first emphasises **people's experience**, their search for truth, their journey towards faith. Both Hinduism and Buddhism fit into this category.

> The second type emphasises God's **revelation of himself** to humankind and humankind's response to God. Judaism, Christianity and Islam are examples of this second type of world religion.

2. Religious sects: religions that separate from the parent or main religion (in Latin, *sectare* means to cut off). While keeping many of the beliefs of the parent religion, they emphasise one aspect in particular. For instance, the Amish community, made famous by the film *Witness*, are Christians, but place special emphasis on living separately from the world.

3. Polytheism: the belief in or the worship of more than one god.

4. Monotheism: the belief in and worship of one god only.

5. Scripture: a sacred or significant book or piece of writing containing some of the key beliefs of a particular religion.

6. Meditation: deep thinking about or reflection on spiritual matters.

7. Shrine: a place that is considered holy because of its association with a sacred object or person.

8. Reincarnation: the belief that after death the soul is born again in another body or form.

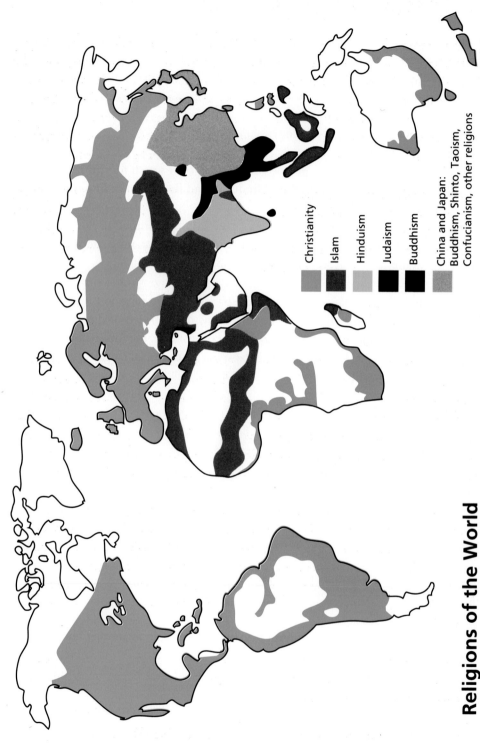

Religions of the World

Approximate distribution of major religions; only the predominant religion in each region has been shown.

Christianity

Islam

Hinduism

Judaism

Buddhism

China and Japan:
Buddhism, Shinto, Taoism,
Confucianism, other religions

Hinduism

Many westerners first became familiar with Hinduism because of the life and influence of Mahatma Gandhi, the great Indian leader and liberator. Gandhi is most famous for his role in obtaining independence for India from British rule in 1947. However, his most lasting impression on the world was his belief in *non-violence* as a method of achieving particular aims. He was not just a political leader of his people, he was also their spiritual guide. So inspiring were his spiritual ideas and his campaign for civil rights that many Christians and non-Christians alike were encouraged to examine the religion he professed.

Gandhi was a Hindu, a believer in the religion professed by 85 per cent of the 700 million people living in India today. This, the oldest of the main world religions, can trace its origins back to 2,000 BC. It has no specific founder, no fixed dogma and no common worship. Indeed, rather than defining it as a single religion, it would be more accurate to see it as an umbrella religion embracing many different forms of the same beliefs.

Main Beliefs

1. Brahman

Hinduism is mainly monotheistic with its belief in Brahman as the supreme god. Other lesser gods rank on a par with our angels and saints. Brahman is not a person, it is a supreme force that is part of every aspect of life and the world. There is nothing that is separated from the sacredness of Brahman or this absolute force. Thus, for example, cows are regarded as sacred and are allowed to roam the streets. They are reminders to the people that Brahman runs through all of creation. Gandhi's non-violent method follows from the belief that Brahman is part of everything and so to attack or kill anything is to attack Brahman.

The divine part of people is called *atman* or the soul. Essentially it is part of Brahman and seeks reunification with Brahman. This reunification is very difficult, however, because most people are blinded by the distractions of this world. Hindus believe that only Brahman is real and everything else is an illusion, or unreal. However, most people get caught up in the illusion of the world and this prevents them from reuniting with Brahman. Thus, this world is seen by Hindus as a place of slavery, a prison that prevents people from achieving their spiritual goal.

This makes Hinduism a very difficult religion to live as not even death can release people from the prison of this world as they undergo numerous rebirths. Hindus hope ultimately for such a release but it is very difficult to achieve.

This understanding of God or Brahman gives rise to two further beliefs:

a. *Karma*: this is the belief that every person is born into the position in life that they have earned in a previous life. So, in a previous life, someone who had lived well, doing good deeds, performing works of devotion and meditation, would come back to a higher form of life. This process of rebirth is called *Samsara*.

b. *Samsara*: what we might call reincarnation. Everyone must go through numerous reincarnations before they achieve salvation or union with Brahman. Moreover, if a person lives a careless or evil life, then he or she can come back as a lower form of life, which includes animal and plant life.

2. The Caste System

Hindus do not just belong to families. They also belong to different classes or castes. Castes are both social and religious divisions. There are four main classes and numerous subdivisions of these. The four main classes are:

> a. Brahmins – the priests and the leaders
> b. Kshatriyas – merchants, farmers, manufacturers, professionals
> c. Vashyas – manual labourers and servants
> d. Harijans – outcasts or 'untouchables'

In previous times, each caste was looked upon as a separate species. These castes could not mix or intermarry. A person was born into a particular caste and had to remain part of that caste until after death when he or she might be reborn into a different caste. In the past there was discrimination against the lower castes.

Today, public discrimination against the lower castes is illegal although the caste system is still very much part of modern India. Before Gandhi was involved with the movement for an independent India, he worked in South Africa, campaigning for human rights for the Harijans or Untouchables. However, from the religious point of view, movement from one caste to another can only take place at the time of death when a person may be born into another, hopefully higher caste. Finally, salvation or union with Brahman can only be achieved through being born into the highest or Brahmin class, or through a second method called *moksha* or liberation.

3. The Hindu paths to salvation

In many respects, Hinduism is a very difficult religion from the point of view of attaining what we call heaven or salvation. It can be very depressing to think that people have to go through so many incarnations, particularly if they are born into one of the lower castes. This has led Hindus to come up with the notion of *moksha*, whereby salvation might be achieved and the cycles of reincarnation ended through one of the following methods:

A. The path of knowledge

This is not knowledge in the purely intellectual sense. It is believed that a person comes to a moment of truth or of insight as a result of deep meditation. This truth is so real and so powerful that not only does the person realise the basic truth of Hindu belief – namely that Brahman is real and everything else is an illusion – but also achieves union with Brahman.

B. The path of devotion

This involves devotion to a particular god. Rather than striving to attain liberation, a person surrenders to a god and allows salvation to take place. In practice, this method involves the worship of such a god in temples, at shrines or at altars in the home. This worship is known as *bhakti.*

C. The path of action

This path is only open to the upper three castes, and only to men. Unlike the previous two paths, this one allows a man to participate in the activities of this world and then go on to seek union with Brahman. So a man of the upper three classes goes through four stages in his life:

Hindu rites

1. Student life: For between ten and twenty years a man is required to study, practise celibacy and perform certain rituals under the guidance of a guru.

2. Marriage: Here the man becomes a householder and his life involves duties towards his family, his community and his caste.

3. Hermit: Once again a man enters a life of celibacy and devotes his life to prayer and meditation.

4. Homeless religious beggar: A man now re-enters society from being a hermit and as a wandering man of prayer and devotion prepares for death and, hopefully, liberation and union with Brahman.

A Hindu at prayer

Hindu Festivals

India has a huge number of festivals. The main ones include:

● Temple Festivals – at least once a year, the temple image is taken on a public procession with great celebration.

● Holi Festival – this is held at the beginning of spring and has its origins in ancient fertility rites.

● Dasera Festival – held in September/October for ten days. It is held in honour of the goddess Dunga.

Hinduism and Christianity

It is obvious that there are many differences between Hinduism and Christianity. Hindus describe God as a force. Christians see him as a person.

The belief in reincarnation and karma is foreign to Christian thinking. Christianity is concerned about the world and about making the world a better place to live in. Hindus see the world as an illusion, therefore denying that the world has been more important for them. However, Gandhi did strive to improve the human condition by seeking civil rights and independence for India, suggesting a certain change in Hindu thinking, and in recent years discrimination on the basis of the caste system has been made illegal.

In recent years too, the western world and its religions have been much enriched by the practice of meditation which has always been important for Hindus.

SUMMARY CHART – HINDUISM

1. Main beliefs	a. Brahman = Supreme god or force b. Atman = Soul, which seeks reunification with Brahman c. Karma = the belief that every person is born into the position in life that they have earned in a previous life. d. Samsara = everyone must go through numerous reincarnations before they achieve union with Brahman.
2. The caste system	a. Castes are both social and religions divisions or classes. b. There are four main castes. c. Movement from one caste to another may only take place at the time of death.

3. The Hindu path to salvation	a. Salvation or union with Brahman is only possible through being born into the highest caste or through
	b. Moksha
	  i. Path of knowledge
	  ii. Path of devotion
	  iii. Path of action

4. Hindu festivals	a. Temple festivals b. Holi festivals c. Dasera festivals

 Revision questions

1. What are the main beliefs of Hinduism?
2. What is the Hindu concept of salvation? How does it compare with the Christian concept of salvation?

Buddhism

India was the land of the birth of Buddhism but today it is mostly practised in South-East Asia, in countries like China, Korea, Vietnam, Nepal, Tibet, Burma and Sri Lanka. In some of these countries, particularly Sri Lanka, Thailand and Burma, Buddhism has become the national religion. The famous Dalai Lama, spiritual leader or head Buddhist monk in Tibet, was exiled by Chinese Communists, and it was this event which aroused western interest in the Buddhist religion. As westerners learned more about the teachings and practices of Buddhism, many of its ideas and exercises began to appeal to them. This is particularly true of Zen Buddhism which is practised in Japan. The style of meditation practiced by Zen Buddhists has particular appeal for many people today who, in a busy world, are attracted by the quiet reflective traditions of this religion. In a world full of noise the experience of silence can be a rare and valued moment.

The origins of Buddhism

Buddhism has its origins in Hinduism. Its story goes back to the sixth century BC to a man named Siddhartha Gautama. Gautama was a Hindu, born into the Brahmin caste. He was part of the warrior group as his father was a chief. His father had great ambitions for him, hoping that he would go on to become an emperor. He tried to protect him from the suffering and hardship of the world by building great palaces for him, giving him a fine education and exposing him to the pleasures of the world. Eventually Gautama married a princess and had a son.

However, despite his upbringing, Gautama was not totally absorbed by the pleasures of the world. Escaping from his sheltered environment he visited a nearby city, where he saw something of the suffering of the world. In the city he met a senile old man, a sick man covered in sores, and he saw a corpse, which was being carried to where it would be cremated. When he looked at the face of the corpse he saw that it was that of a wandering religious beggar (the fourth stage in the path of action). There was such an expression of peace and joy on his face that Gautama was deeply moved. More than that, the experience raised fundamental questions for him concerning suffering and death and the meaning of life.

He decided to leave his family and become a hermit. He lived the most rigid life, imposing harsh disciplines on his body. He was almost at death's door when he realised that this cruel life was not getting him anywhere. He abandoned this way of life and went to meditate under a Bo tree by the river Gaya. As a result he became *enlightened*, or gained insight into the meaning of suffering and the path to salvation. His insight was that all of human existence is subject to the experience of suffering. Suffering is caused by desire and the only way that this problem can be tackled is by following a middle way between a life of pleasure and a life of total denial. As a result of this 'discovery' Gautama became known as the 'enlightened one' or the 'Buddha'.

Gautama then went to preach his first sermon to five of his former companions. These five companions became his first disciples and the first Buddhist order of monks. These monks would travel for eight months of the year from place to place and would spend the rest of the year, the rainy season, in bamboo huts which were given to them by wealthy followers. For the rest of his life, Gautama travelled India preaching his message. He died in 483 BC at the age of eighty.

Buddhist teachings

1. The middle way

In one way it could be said that Buddhism emerged because the Hindu path to salvation was too difficult. Gautama's middle way seemed a more realistic option. He rejected the idea of reincarnation, that one had to pass through numerous rebirths before one achieved salvation. Instead he taught that salvation was possible within one's lifetime.

2. Nirvana

Nirvana is the goal of human existence, a state of total bliss that one arrives at when desire ceases and the struggle ends. Once people let go of their desires, the needs of the false self, they will achieve nirvana. This is the conclusion that Gautama reached following his 'discovery' of what he called the Four Noble Truths.

The Four Noble Truths

1. All life is suffering: this does not mean just physical suffering but the human frustration of never being able to get our lives together, never being able to attain total peace.

2. The cause of suffering is desire or clinging. What makes suffering so much part of life is that everything passes. Nothing is lasting – youth, good health, happiness. We cling to things, our possessions, the people we love, our joys, our very lives, in the hope that they will last but the truth is that all will pass.

3. Suffering can be overcome by abandoning the desire to cling. When we become enlightened and see life for what it is, when we let go of our desire, we overcome suffering and achieve nirvana.

4. Nirvana can be attained by following the way of wisdom, morality and meditation as outlined in the eightfold path.

1. Right understanding: this sees life as changing and pain. The false self must be understood and rejected.
2. Right thoughts: this includes the spirit of good will and denial of what is false.
3. Right speech: gossip, lies and slander must be avoided.
4. Right action: killing, stealing and sexual immorality must be avoided.
5. Right means of livelihood: religion must be part of daily life and work. Therefore one must work well and avoid activities that are harmful to animals or people, for example the production of alcoholic drink, the sale of arms, the slaughter of animals.
6. Right effort: the false self is always tempting one to engage in wrong thoughts and feelings. Therefore a constant effort is required to achieve the wisdom of Buddha.
7. Right mindfulness: attention must always be paid to the present moment and to inner thoughts and impulses.
8. Right concentration: meditation helps to concentrate the mind and focus it on what is important.

Like Hinduism, Buddhism does not put a great emphasis on the salvation of the world. Buddhism, with its emphasis on meditation, is much more concerned with salvation *from the world*. Like Christianity, it does offer a way of salvation but it is modelled on an eight-fold path rather than on a person as Christian salvation is. Christian salvation is concerned with freedom from sin, evil and death in the peace which is God's gift in the Risen Christ. Buddhism is much more about the mind and being enlightened. It is, therefore, more 'inner wordly' and 'other wordly'. Yet Christianity can admire the emphasis in Buddhism on enlightened thinking and on the practice of meditation.

SUMMARY CHART – BUDDHISM

1 Origins of Buddhism	Buddha (Enlightened One)
2 Buddhist Teachings	a. The Middle Way = Path to Salvation b. Nirvana is the goal of human existence c. The Four Noble Truths d. The Eightfold Path

Revision questions
1. Why do you think the Buddha is known as the 'Enlightened One'?
2. Why does meditation play such an important role in Buddhism?

The former religious and secular leader of Tibet, the Dalai Lama is regarded as the spiritual leader of Tibetan Buddhists. Since the Chinese takeover of Tibet, the Dalai Lama has lived in exile in India.

Islam is the youngest of the world religions. Like Judaism and Christianity, it finds its roots in the Near East. Like Judaism and Christianity also, it claims Abraham as its Father. Abraham's constant theme was that of a divine promise of a glorious future. These three religions take the ideas of Promise and of Future very seriously. Because Abraham was a prophet who proclaimed these ideas which are so central to Judaism, Christianity and Islam, these are called prophetic religions.

The Origins of Islam – The Prophet Muhammad

Islam as a religion was born almost six hundred years after the birth of Jesus, and into that same prophetic religion of hope from which Christianity sprang. While it accepts the promise of the father Abraham, its specific origin lies with the Prophet Muhammad, who was born in the city of Mecca in Arabia about 570 AD.

Muhammad was orphaned at the age of six and spent his childhood with a succession of relatives. Even as a child it is said that he was very religious. He spent much of his time with both Jews and Christians who told him many of their religious stories.

Back in Mecca, Muhammad was disgusted by many of the corruptions he found there. There was great inequality, unwanted female babies were buried alive, merchants made fortunes by selling idols and sacrificial animals to poor people, who worshipped many gods.

At the age of twenty-five, Muhammad was proposed to by a wealthy widow of forty with whom he had six children. When he was middle-aged himself, he began to spend time wandering the hills in deep reflection, particularly on the subject of death. At the age of forty, he received a revelation from God calling on him to denounce the polytheism and paganism of Mecca, and to preach the existence of one God, Allah. This revelation would change both his future and that of the world. Muhammad would become a prophet for Allah.

The Hijra
In the early years, Muhammad had few followers (named Companions); a turning-point came in July 622 when he was asked by the citizens of Medina to leave Mecca and come to their city, located 400 kilometres north of Mecca. This event is known as the *Hijra,* meaning departure or exodus, and it marks the beginning of the Muslim calendar. In Medina, Muhammad began to spread his message. He also became the political and military leader. The leaders in Mecca wanted to crush Islam while Muhammad wanted to convert the people of Mecca from their wicked ways. Eventually, after he had won three major battles, Muhammad went directly to the *Kaaba* in Mecca, the main shrine for the worship of idols. He believed that this shrine should be dedicated to the worship of one God, and so he had

all the idols destroyed. The only thing preserved was a black stone, a meteorite that was said to have been given to Abraham by the angel Gabriel. This became a sacred stone. Later the Kaaba became a place of pilgrimage for devout Muslims.

Huge numbers of people began converting to Islam. Muhammad believed that the State and religion should be one; by the time he died in 632 he had united the Arab tribes in a *theocracy* – a State governed by the will of God who acts through leaders who believe that they have been inspired by God. Muhammad was succeeded as leader by a series of caliphs (successors). Muslims see the role of prophets as very important, the most important being Abraham, Moses, Noah, Jesus and, finally, Muhammad himself, who they believe was given the final and the fullest revelation of God, and who is called the *seal of the prophets*. None of these prophets, not even Jesus or Muhammad, is seen as divine. They are simply messengers of the one, true God.

The Qur'an (Koran)

The **Qur'an** is the Muslim sacred book. Muslims believe that it is the Word of God, exactly as the Angel Gabriel revealed it to Muhammad. Muhammad himself could not write so he had people write it down for him. After his death many Muslims were killed in battle, and one of his early companions, Abu Bakr, was afraid that the **Qur'an** might be lost so he had a copy made which was completed less than two years after Muhammad died. It is written in Arabic. Muslims believe that the **Qur'an** is the infallible Word of God sent down from heaven to Muhammad and nothing can change it. Hence Muslims show great reverence for this book. They read it every day. Many learn parts of it by heart. Its essential message is that God created the world and everything in it. It also contains a complete set of rules for everyday life.

Muslims also read the *Hadith* – the story of the life of Muhammad and the early Muslim communities.

Basic Islamic beliefs

1. GOD – ALLAH – Muslims believe there is only one God, Allah. His existence is not questioned. He is God and all powerful. They pray every day to Allah. 'There is no God but God and Muhammad is his messenger.' Thus, Islam is a monotheistic religion.

2. ANGELS – The Koran strongly professes the existence of angels. They are God's messengers who bring God's messages to the prophets, as for example by the Angel Gabriel to the prophet Muhammad. Some angels spend their time keeping an account of human behaviour.

3. THE DAY OF JUDGMENT – On the last day, people will be raised to life and will appear before God to be sent to heaven or hell, depending on how they have lived their lives. It is not the effects of people's actions that matter, it is their intentions.

The central beliefs and practices of Islam are called the Five Pillars of Faith.

1. THE CREED, or confession of faith 'There is no God but God, and Muhammad is the messenger of God.' Muslims must recite and believe this creed.
2. PRAYER: Muslims pray five times daily – at daybreak, noon, mid-afternoon, just after sunset and early in the night. They may pray alone, with others, or in the mosque. At these times, criers (*muezzins*) call people to prayer. There is a highly elaborate ritual attached to such prayer. Muslims always pray facing Mecca. On Fridays, there are special prayers for men only at noon. In the mosques there are prayer rugs which cover the floors. There are no statues as Muslims believe that they become idols.
3. FASTING: During the ninth month, called *Ramadan*, Muslims must not eat, drink or have sexual relations between dawn and sunset. This is to encourage obedience to God and care for the needy.
4. ALMSGIVING: Muslims must give at least 2.5% of their income to charity.
5. PILGRIMAGE: Muslims are expected to go to Mecca at least once in their lifetime. This pilgrimage is called *Hajj*. Non-Muslims can neither make this pilgrimage nor enter Mecca. The pilgrimage takes place during the twelfth month. The male pilgrims wear white robes as a sign of their equality before God. Women must be covered from head to toe.

Islam in Ireland

Muslims began arriving in Ireland in the early 1950s, many to study in the Royal College of Surgeons in Dublin. In 1959 the Dublin Islamic Society was formed by a group of Muslim students. As the Muslim population of Dublin grew, the Dublin Islamic Society recognised the need for a permanent Mosque and Islamic centre. The first Mosque in Ireland was opened in Harrington Street in Dublin in 1975.

During the 1980s the Muslim community continued to grow, and in 1983 the present Mosque and Islamic Centre on the South Circular Road was opened. However the Muslim community is increasing so much that these facilities are already being seen as too small.

Today there are over six thousand Muslims in Ireland, the majority of whom live in Dublin. There are small mosques in Cork, Galway and Ballyhaunis, Co. Mayo. On 24 April 1992 President Mary Robinson opened the first recognised Muslim school in Ireland and Britain. Among the enrolment for 1993 were Bosnian refugees who were brought to Ireland by the Irish Government.

In September 1993 *The Irish Times* interviewed some Muslims living in Ireland.

Ali Abbas is from the Punjab area of Pakistan, like many Irish Pakistanis. He left home in the 1970s to study mechanical engineering in England, and came to Ireland to spend a holiday with his brother. Most Pakistani emigration to the city has been 'chain migration' of family groups and much of it has been a spill-over from Britain.

'I found Ireland was like a home', says Ali Abbas. 'It was a nice country.'

He went into the clothing business, one of the favoured trades for Pakistanis here, but as the community grew, he saw a gap in the market for a shop selling food from the Muslim world. In his seductive, aromatic shop, Indian specialities like Tandoori paste and Madras paste, split mung beans and coconut milk jostle with the more Mediterranean favourites of the Arab community, and even the palm oil, melon seeds and potato flower beloved of Nigerians. Ali Abbas first saw his wife on his wedding day, and when I joke that he must have been crossing his fingers that he'd get a looker, he grows serious: 'The main thing is inside, the outside doesn't matter. I realised that the first day of marriage. The main thing was, to have respect for each other, and to have no lies or cheating. That's the real meaning of love.'

'It is a very, very serious problem, especially in Ireland, because there are so many problems about which religion the children will have.'

Zoubir was brought to Ireland 18 years ago by Dublin Meat Packers as the country's first ritual slaughterer for Halal Meats.

With the youngest two of his four children somersaulting over his knees as he speaks, Zoubir explains that his marriage – arranged, as is the custom in the Muslim world – has worked out well: 'I think there is more divorce when you meet your wife just somewhere, than when you meet her through your family.' he says.

'And if you spend four years together before you marry, you know each other very well, and the fights start.' He adds philosophically, however: 'Marriage is like you are playing cards, and there is separation and divorce all over the world.'

Arranged marriages mean that most Muslims settled in Ireland will have a partner chosen for them in the home country, or in the wider British Muslim community.

Islam and Christianity

Both Islam and Christianity share a belief in one God, the resurrection of the dead and the importance of prayer, fasting and almsgiving. The essential difference between Islam and Christianity centres on Jesus Christ. While Christians believe that Jesus was the Son of God, our Saviour who died and rose again, Muslims regard Jesus simply as a great prophet who was not divine. They regard Muhammad as God's greatest and final prophet. Christians, on the other hand, do not accept Muhammad as a prophet.

SUMMARY CHART – ISLAM	
1. Origins of Islam	Prophet Muhammad City of Mecca
2. Holy Book	Qu'ran
3. Basic Islamic Beliefs	a. Allah – God b. Angels c. Day of Judgment
4. Central beliefs and practices of Islam	The Five Pillars 1. Creed 2. Prayer 3. Fasting 4. Almsgiving 5. Pilgrimage

Revision questions
1. What are the Five Pillars of Islam?
2. How does Islam compare with Christianity?

CHAPTER 9

Judaism

This chapter considers the religion of the Jewish people which is called Judaism. It shows that the history of the Jews is also the story of their religious faith even up to the present day.

Introduction

Judaism is the religion of the Jewish people. It is the religion of a nation – God's chosen people. Yet today, while there are twelve million Jews in the world, only two million live in Israel, the land of their Fathers. There are six million Jews living in the US and four million more scattered around the world, many of them in Russia and eastern Europe.

For most people in the western world, their awareness of Judaism and of the Jews is keener than that of other world religions. As a religion Judaism holds special significance for Christians since the God of Abraham, Isaac and Jacob is their God too, and they claim the Hebrew Scriptures as their Old Testament.

Early history

The early history of the Jews – their national and religious story – is told in the Hebrew Bible, in particular the first five books of the Bible, known as the PENTATEUCH.

Abraham was the Father of the Jewish people and it was he who first led a people who were wandering nomads in the desert to settle down in the land of Canaan. From then on, as the time-line shows, the Jews experienced much conquest in their history. They spent time in exile in Egypt and in Babylon. They were conquered by neighbouring empires like the Assyrians, the Persians, the Greeks and the Romans who destroyed their Temple in 70 AD. The Wailing Wall is all that remains of this Temple in Jerusalem today and it is a place of pilgrimage for Jews all over the world.

The history of the Jews is the history of their religion

The history of the Jewish people cannot be studied without at the same time studying the history of God's involvement with them – his revelation of himself to them. Their history is at one and the same time their faith story. Everything that happens to them as a people and as a nation is interpreted in the light of God's presence and action with his people. Thus, as we trace the history of the Jewish people we also trace the history of their religious belief.

ABRAHAM So we begin with Abraham, a wandering nomad who survived the deserts of the Near East by transporting his family from one place to another.

From the biblical account we see that Abraham was called by God to settle in the land of Canaan. 'Go from your country and your people and your father's house to the land that I will show you. And I will make of you a great nation...' *(Gen 12: 1-1)*. 'And I will give to you and to your descendants after you, the land of your sojournings, all the land of Canaan, for an everlasting possession; and I will be their God' *(Gen 17:8)*.

The Jewish religion emerges as a nation religion and as a prophetic religion – a people in their land responding to an invitation or a call to trust themselves to the promise of the future.

> And I will establish my covenant between me and you
> and your descendants after you throughout their nations
> for an everlasting covenant. *(Gen 17:6)*

A covenant is an agreement between two people. The covenant described in Genesis is based on the promise by God that Abraham would be the father of a nation, that this nation would have a land of its own and that through this nation all the nations of the earth would find blessing.

It is in this sense that the Jews can be described as the CHOSEN PEOPLE. They are not a 'chosen people' in an unfair way that would leave others out. Rather they are chosen to carry out a task, to bring God's message to all nations.

Abraham was called to put his trust in God.

Let us consider for a moment what is involved here. When we trust someone we take a certain risk. We do not know with scientific certainty that our trust is not misplaced or will not be betrayed. We take that step of trust in the hope that we are doing the right thing. This was what Abraham must have experienced, making Judaism a religion of promise or revelation (God) and trust or faith (human response).

MOSES The Jewish story continues with the Jews seeking refuge in Egypt because of famine in Canaan and then becoming slaves in Egypt. Having spent over four hundred years as slaves in Egypt they were led out of Egypt by Moses in an event known as the Exodus. Once again we realise that the Jews saw the hand of God in the events of history. 'Yahweh heard our voice and saw our misery, our toil and our oppression; and Yahweh brought us out of Egypt with mighty hand and outstretched arms, with great terror and with signs and wonders. He brought us here and gave us this land, a land where milk and honey flow' (Deuteronomy 26:5-9). In the desert God once again makes a covenant with the Jews: 'I will be your God and you will be my people.' They would be his people by turning away from false Gods and placing their faith in God (Yahweh) alone. The Ten Commandments given at Mount Sinai spell out how the Jews could turn away from slavery to false gods and trust in the one true God.

The struggle to abandon idolatry and place their trust in God becomes the major challenge of Jewish faith. As we learn the history of the Jews from the time they settled in the Promised Land, through the various attacks on them by the Assyrians, Babylonians, Greeks and Romans, the struggle to remain faithful to God is a constant theme. This was because the fulfilment of God's promise always seemed too far off, whereas the attractions of the present could give immediate satisfaction. This is often our experience too. So prophets rose up urging the people to trust in the promise.

The Prophets

The prophets were not magical people with visions of the future. Rather they served as voices to tell the people how far they had strayed from being God's people. It is no coincidence that they were most prominent when times were good and the people forgot about their relationship with God. We can well understand this today when we observe that religious faith seems to decline in times and places of prosperity and material well-being. So prophets like Amos, Hosea, Isaiah and Micah spoke out against injustice and paganism. They were not afraid to tell their kings that prosperity and political success did not necessarily mean that they were fulfilling their side of the covenant. We find an example of this with Elijah the Prophet who condemned King Ahab and his wife Jezebel for supporting two cults – Baal and Astarte. So the prophets were in many ways the conscience of the people.

The prophet Micah sums up what was demanded of God's followers:

> 'This is what the Lord asks of you, only this: to act justly, to love tenderly, and to walk humbly with your God.' (Micah 6:8)

The hope for a Messiah

The hope for a messiah begins with the reign of King David. In 2 Samuel 7 we read that David was concerned that the Ark of the Covenant was kept in a tent. The Ark was a movable chest which contained the Ten Commandments, the staff of Aaron and a container of manna from the days of wandering in the desert searching for the Promised Land. The Ark was brought from place to place while the Jews fought many enemies. David wanted to build a house for the Ark and told the prophet Nathan about it. God, speaking through Nathan, told David that he would build a 'house' for David – not a building but a dynasty, God's kingdom on earth which would endure forever.

Belief in the promise of the kingdom became known as 'messianism'. It was largely born out of the Jewish struggle to keep their side of the Covenant and their constant failure to do so. The Messiah would be the one who would show the way. Gradually, however, this concept of a Messiah became a nationalistic and political one as the Jews struggled for independence against a succession of invaders. This explains why the Jews did not accept Jesus as the Messiah. Many Jews expected a political leader who would drive the Romans out of Israel and so enable the Jews to live as an independent people in their homeland.

Other characteristics of Judaism
Worship – Temple – Synagogues – Home

It was David's son, Solomon, who built the temple in Jerusalem. Jerusalem became both the political and religious capital for the Jews. It was their 'holy place', the place of worship for the nation.

Priests became very important in Jerusalem as worship became more and more formal. The Temple was destroyed by the Babylonians when they captured the Southern Kingdom. Many Jews ended up as exiles in Babylon. Later, as a result of Greek and Roman conquests,

Jewish groups settled in parts of the Greek and Roman Empires. They became known as Jews of the Diaspora (dispersal). Synagogues became very important as local places of worship. The word synagogue comes from the Greek word meaning assembly.

So, for the Jews, the synagogue is more than the building – it is the gathering of people, especially for the Sabbath. It is thus the centre of public worship and social life for the Jewish community. At the end facing Jerusalem is placed the Ark containing scrolls of the law. During the service men normally wear skull-caps on their heads and white prayer shawls on their shoulders. Women wear hats but no shawls and in more traditional or orthodox synagogues they are obliged to sit apart from the men. The most important part of the service is when the Ark is opened and the scroll of the Law is taken out and carried around the synagogue.

While the synagogue holds a special place in the religious life of Jews, the centre of their religious life is the home. This is because the family is considered very important. Saturday is their Sabbath and since the Jewish day begins at sundown, the Sabbath begins on Friday evening. A meal with bread and wine is the main point of Sabbath observance. In addition to the keeping of the Sabbath as a day of rest and of worship Jews pray three times daily and keep strict laws on diet which means eating only food which is considered to be clean – Kosher.

The Torah – Law

The Jewish attitude towards the law has its origins both in the Covenant, when God makes his promise and we respond, and in the Jewish experience of the Diaspora – of being scat-

tered. The law going back to the time of Moses is seen as a way of responding to God as shown by God himself. The keeping of this law would bring about the coming of God's kingdom or rule on earth.

The Jews' link with their history also became important and so they began to collect and study the writings of their ancestors. By 400 BC they had collected most of what were to become the Jewish scriptures. The first five books of the Jewish Bible became known as the Torah which means 'law' or 'instruction'. These books contain ancient laws going back to the time of Moses and including the Ten Commandments. They are central to Jewish life. Ultimately the law consists of 613 commandments which are binding on Jews. They concern worship and rules for religious and moral living.

Jewish Festivals

1. Passover: an eight-day festival celebrated in spring, commemorating the Exodus the Israelites' deliverance from slavery in Egypt.
2. Pentecost: celebrated seven weeks after Passover to mark the end of the corn harvest.
3. Tabernacles: celebrated in autumn for the fruit harvest. The celebration includes camping out in booths (tabernacles) which are made of branches. It commemorates the Israelites' journey through the desert.
4. Dedication (Hannukah: the Festival of Lights): celebrated in winter – commemorates the rededication of the second temple in Jerusalem.
5. Purim: held in early spring to mark the deliverance of the Jews of the Persian Empire.
6. New Year: held in early autumn – marks the beginning of the Jewish religious calendar. It is a time of reflection on life and for making new resolutions.
7. Day of Atonement (Yom Kippur): the tenth day of the New Year and the most important of all Jewish holy days. It involves twenty-four hours' abstinence from food and water.

Sacred Writings

1. BIBLE: a collection of books written over a thousand years

2. TORAH: or 'law' – laid down in the first five books of the Bible which are attributed to Moses; spells out how Jews should live

3. MISHNAH (Second century AD): moral teaching based on the Bible

4. TALMUD: contains further reflections on Jewish life

Judaism in the last two thousand years

It was largely because the Muslims conquered their homeland that many Jews left and moved into Christian Europe. In some instances they were invited in by Christian leaders because they could engage in money-lending, which was a proscribed activity for Christians.

Almost from the very beginning Jews were to be victims of what is known as *anti-semitism* (Jews are the Semite people of the Near East). Anti-semitism was to take many forms. From their earliest times in Europe, many Jews were forced to live in *ghettos*, which were special sections of cities, and frequently the poorest. To distinguish them from Christians, they often had to wear yellow badges or distinctive hats. When the Crusaders crossed Europe on their way to the Holy Land to fight the Muslims they frequently attacked Jewish ghettos, causing the Jews to leave and settle in countries like Poland. Much of Poland was taken over by Russia in the late eighteenth century. This brought increasing persecution of the Jews, particularly between 1881 and 1921, in a series of slaughters which became known as *pogroms*. Many of those who survived fled to America and began the increase in the Jewish population of the US.

We are only too familiar with the extremes to which anti-semitism was taken during the period of the Third Reich, from the enactment of the Nuremberg Laws in 1936, depriving the Jews of basic civil rights, to the infamous Kristallnacht (Night of Glass) and the horror of the Holocaust.

The Holocaust itself posed many questions for Jews. How could a good God have allowed this to happen? Why such suffering? As a result some have turned away from the faith. Others see the Holocaust as the product of human free will which is capable of evil, while there are those who see it as a punishment for their sins.

The Creation of the State of Israel

In the late 1880s a movement called Zionism was founded with the aim of setting up a Jewish homeland. Palestine had been Muslim since its conquest over a thousand years earlier. After the First World War the Zionists succeeded in persuading the British (who had a mandate over the region at the time) to allow the immigration of Jews to Palestine. In 1948 the State of Israel was created out of Palestine. This has created much tension between the Jews and their neighbouring Arab states.

The creation of the State of Israel was very significant for the Jews. Once again they were a nation – God's nation. For Jews outside of Palestine, their cry, 'Next year in Jerusalem', has concrete meaning.

CHAPTER 10

Christianity

This chapter looks at Christianity as a world religion. It considers the founder of Christianity, the key beliefs and practices of Christianity and the spread of Christianity, from its beginnings up to the Reformation.

Introduction

Christianity is the largest of the world's religions. Over a billion people around the world acknowledge Jesus Christ as the Son of God and accept him as their Saviour. Christianity is so widespread and is so familiar to us in western Europe that we often take for granted its significance in the world over the last two thousand years. Almost every aspect of civilisation, including art, literature and the law, has been influenced by Christianity. Indeed, the history of Europe is tied in with the history of Christianity in many ways.

Familiarity can sometimes breed apathy and boredom. We may presume at times that we know all that there is to know about Christianity and enjoy more the novelty of considering the other world religions. This may be particularly true since we find ourselves born into Christianity and sometimes think that it has been 'foisted' upon us. It may be difficult for us then to be objective about Christianity. On the other hand, it does mean that we have a unique insight into what it means to be a Christian. Indeed, as we have already suggested, it is truly impossible to come to the heart of any religion without taking that leap of faith. In this chapter, however, we will view Christianity from outside as a world religion set alongside the other major world religions.

The founder of Christianity

We have already seen that many world religions speak of a founder, an enlightened one to whom they look for answers to the riddle of human existence. Buddhism looks to Siddhartha Gautama, while Muslims consider Muhammad to be their supreme prophet. Christians take their name from Jesus Christ, a Jew born in Judaea around 6-4BC. There is some independent historical evidence for the existence of Jesus.

1. The Roman historian **Tacitus** wrote about the great fire which swept through the city of Rome in 64 AD. It was believed that the Roman Emperor, Nero, had started the fire and he successfully shifted the blame on to the Christians in Rome. Tacitus wrote about this group who got their name from Christ.

   > Christians.... suffered the extreme penalty during the reign of Tiberias at the hands of our prosecutors, Pontius Pilate, and a most mischievous superstition, thus checked for the moment, again broke out not only in Judaea, the first source of the evil, but even in Rome, where all things hideous and shameful from every part of the world find their centre and become popular.

2. **Pliny the Younger,** another Roman, helps to confirm the existence of early Christianity and its founder. He was a Roman legate in Asia Minor and he wrote to the Emperor, Trajan, complaining about the growth of Christianity and advising him how to deal with the spread of this religious group. In the letter, he described how the pagan temples were no longer in use and that those who sold animals for pagan sacrifices were experiencing economic difficulty. He advised the Emperor to free any accused Christians who would renounce Christianity and worship pagan gods. He also described how Christians met on a certain day before sunrise, made a prayer to Christ 'as to a god', pledged to keep the law and shared a simple meal.

3. **Josephus** was a Jewish historian of the first century who wrote a twenty-volume history of the Jews, *Jewish Antiquities*, in which he describes Judaea under the rule of Pontius Pilate.

   > Now, there was about this time, a wise man, if it is lawful to call him a man, for he was a doer of wonderful works, a teacher of such men as receive the truth with pleasure. He drew over to him both many of the Jews, and many of the Gentiles. He was the Christ. And when Pilate, at the suggestion of the principal men among us, had condemned him to the cross, those that loved him at first did not forsake him; as the divine prophets had foretold these and ten thousand other wonderful things concerning him. And the tribe of Christians so named after him are not extinct at this day.

Although some scholars doubt the objectivity of Josephus' account, suggesting that he himself was a Christian and therefore biased, the fact is that he did not question the historical existence of Jesus.

The New Testament is, however, our primary source of knowledge about Jesus and his message. Through it we learn that he grew up in Galilee and that he began what is called his public life at the age of thirty, when he was baptised by John the Baptist who proclaimed his coming. We learn that he gathered the apostles around him and spent the next three years preaching, teaching and healing the sick. He proclaimed the kingdom of God and called on people to repent. He died by crucifixion at the age of thirty-three at the hands of the Romans. His followers claim that he rose from the dead three days later, appearing to different people. Forty days later he ascended to his father in heaven.

Jesus' life, death and resurrection have become the central beliefs of Christianity. He is viewed on the one hand as God's ultimate revelation of himself to humankind and on the other hand as the perfect human response to God's revelation. In this sense he has become the way to God for all Christians.

Christianity as a prophetic religion

We have already looked at two prophetic religions, Judaism and Islam. Chronologically, Christianity stands as the second of these prophetic religions, coming after Judaism, which began almost two thousand years before Christ, and before Islam which dates from the sixth century AD. Christianity is rooted in Judaism and thus traces its history back to Abraham and the idea of future fulfilment in which the Jews professed belief.

Jesus as prophet

For Christians, Jesus is the one in a long line of prophets who proved to be of ultimate significance. To the belief of Abraham and of Moses – the belief in the future promise – his preaching gave a unique insight – God was a loving father – **Abba**. So certain did Jesus appear to be about this and so intimate seemed his knowledge of and relationship with God that he began to be accused of blasphemy. His way of communicating God's love was by being with those in society most in need of it – lepers, tax-collectors, prostitutes. He was more than the prophet proclaiming God's promise. Those who came to believe in him, those who were to call themselves Christians, saw his person and his life as the total manifestation of God's love. In this way they could not think about God without thinking about Jesus too. Ultimately they began to see him as the 'Son of God' – the one who fulfilled God's promise to be with his people. His resurrection from the dead became the basis of their hope.

Christianity – Key Beliefs

The truth central to Christianity concerns God the Father, Jesus Christ and the Holy Spirit transforming human history and the world. This truth is expressed in what have become known as creeds: the Apostles' Creed which is used in the western Church and the Nicene Creed which dates from 325 AD and is used in the Church worldwide.

We believe in one God,
the Father, the almighty,
maker of heaven and earth,
of all that is, seen and unseen.
We believe in one Lord, Jesus Christ,
the only Son of God,
eternally begotten of the Father,
God from God, Light from Light,
true God from true God,
begotten, not made,
of one being with the Father.
Through him all things were made.
For us men and for our salvation
he came down from heaven:
by the power of the Holy Spirit,
he became incarnate from the Virgin Mary, and was made man.
For our sake he was crucified under Pontius Pilate;
he suffered death and was buried.
On the third day he rose again
in accordance with the Scriptures;
he ascended into heaven
and is seated at the right hand of the Father.
He will come again in glory to judge the living and the dead,
and his kingdom will have no end.
We believe in the Holy Spirit, the Lord, the giver of life,
who proceeds from the Father and the son.
With the Father and the Son he is worshipped and glorified.
 He has spoken through the Prophets.
We believe in one holy catholic and apostolic Church.
We acknowledge one baptism for the forgiveness of sins.
We look for the resurrection of the dead,
and the life of the world to come. Amen.

The Christian Way

In our study of Judaism we saw that the Jews' way of responding to God's promise was spelt out in the Ten Commandments. The keeping of these precepts or laws became so important in Jewish thinking that they spelt them out in further laws and sub-laws. By Jesus' time, many Jews had become very legalistic. Indeed, Jesus told the story of the Good Samaritan as a way of chiding the Jews for emphasising the letter of the law while losing sight of its spirit. He summarised the law in two commandments.

The first commandment is this: 'Hear, O Israel, the Lord, our God, is the only Lord. You shall love the Lord your God with all your heart, with all your soul, with all your mind, and with all your strength.'

The second is this:

'Love your neighbour as yourself.' There is no greater commandment than these.

When the disciples asked Jesus to teach them to pray, he taught them the 'Our Father' – again a summary of Christian belief and living.

Our Father, who art in heaven,
hallowed be thy name.
Thy kingdom come.
Thy will be done on earth, as it is in heaven.
Give us this day our daily bread,
and forgive us our trespasses,
as we forgive those who trespass against us,
and lead us not into temptation,
but deliver us from evil.

Ivory figurine of a gladiator, from South Shields, England. Courtesy Museum of Antiquities, Newcastle upon Tyne.

Early Christianity

Christianity was born when the Roman Empire was at the height of its power. Roman rule extended north as far as Britain, south into North Africa and east into Turkey, Palestine, Egypt and Syria. From one point of view, life under Roman rule seemed very progressive. There was peace over a vast area, so trade and agriculture prospered. There was time for the development of literature and the arts. Towns grew with their theatres, law courts and temples. Roman skill at road-making made communication very easy. Latin was the official language, although Greek was spoken in places like Greece and Egypt.

From the religious point of view, things were very different. Most people were still pagans, believing in a myriad gods. Superstition was rampant. As often happened, when the people became wealthier they become more corrupt, so that adultery, prostitution and drunkenness were the order of the day. As the craving for entertainment and pleasure grew, the arenas with their gladiator fights became hugely popular. Palestine was one exception within this huge Roman Empire. Here, people had come to believe in one God and had developed a concept of justice and morality, even if they did not always put this into practice. However, most Jews did not accept that Jesus was the long-awaited Messiah. They were expecting a more political leader who would help free them from Roman rule. So Christianity was born into a world which was either pagan or which viewed it as heresy.

148

The growth of the Christian Church began on the day of Pentecost when St Peter preached to the Jews in Jerusalem and three thousand people were baptised. Born as it was in Palestine and preached as it was by those who were once Jews caused Christianity to be considered a part of Judaism for a while. Christianity for the most part was not accepted in Palestine. Through the work of its missionaries it spread to the Mediterranean areas of the Roman Empire. Everywhere these missionaries went, they set up communities of believers called 'churches' – so we end up with the church at Corinth, the church at Ephesus, the church at Rome. The way of life of these early Christians and the challenge of the Christian message became unacceptable to many Romans with their pagan gods and corrupt lifestyles. Moreover, these Christians were actually preaching the message of a man who had been executed by the Romans. So the persecution of Christians began around 64 AD during the reign of the Emperor Nero. Both Peter and Paul died during these early persecutions. However as we have often seen during the course of history (the Penal times in Ireland, communist rule in Russia), Christianity survived and, indeed, continued to attract new converts.

Characteristics of early Christianity

1. **The Catechumenate** Becoming a Christian was not as easy or as automatic as it seems today. Despite the desire for converts a lengthy preparation was compulsory for would-be Christians. The Eucharist was the centre of Christianity but before a person was admitted to the Eucharist, he or she had to learn what it meant to be a Christian. So the catechumen (learner) was instructed on the story of salvation from the time of Abraham up to Jesus, on the Apostles' Creed, on Christian morality and on prayer. Then he or she spent a period of

The Roman Colosseum

time (Lent) praying and fasting. Only when the community was satisfied that the catechumen was ready to become a fully-fledged Christian was he or she baptised. It is interesting to note, however, that living with the Christian community and sharing the life of faith came before learning about that faith. Knowledge about Christian faith only made sense within the context of a life of Christian faith.

2. **Ecclesia (Church)** Church buildings as we know them did not exist in the early Christian Church. They could not build churches for a hunted and persecuted people. 'Church', therefore, meant the community of believers either locally or throughout the world. Early Christian worship took place in private houses and in secret.

3. **The Church Fathers** In his book *The Christian Heritage,* Fr Desmond Forristal points to the significance of the early Christian writers.

> By the middle of the second century, the Christians were beginning to defend themselves against their enemies. Christian writers were setting down what they believed and showing how untrue were the accusations made against them. The writers of these early times are of great importance, since they bear witness to the beliefs of the first Christians and are so close in time to the apostles and to Jesus himself. The main writers of the first six centuries or so are generally known as the Fathers of the Church, because of the part they played in shaping the life and thought of the Christian Church.

These writers included Justin, Ignatius, Irenaeus, Tertullian and Cyprian.

A Eucharistic celebration, from a painting in the catacomb of St Callistus

4. The Centrality of the Eucharist The centre of early Christian life was the Eucharist. St Justin, one of the Fathers of the Church, describes a Sunday Eucharist in Rome about the year 150 AD.

> This celebration of the Eucharist on Sunday, the day of Resurrection, was a distinguishing characteristic of early Christianity. On the one hand it marked the break from Judaism – Saturday was the Jewish Sabbath. On the other hand it was viewed as the high point of Christianity. Only baptised Christians were allowed to participate.

The Spread of Christianity

1. The Christian Empire

313 AD was a turning-point for Christianity. In that year Constantine became the Emperor of Rome and, with the edict of Milan, he put an end to the laws against Christians and allowed freedom of religion throughout the Empire. His successors made Christianity the official religion of the Roman Empire.

Some features of Christianity at this time

A. The conversion of the Emperor, coupled with the fact that the Roman Empire was so vast, helped the rapid spread of Christianity throughout Europe and Northern Africa as well as Russia and Eastern Asia.

B. The fact that Christianity could be practised more openly and freely meant that the structure of the Christian Church became more definite. Diocesan and parochial structures developed and the celebration of the Eucharist moved from people's homes to churches which were modelled on the Roman basilicas. There were two reasons for this more ordered structure to Christianity. Firstly, an increase in numbers always calls for more structure and organisation. Secondly, the Roman desire for order and uniformity influenced Christianity as it developed in the Roman Empire.

C. Constantine moved the capital of the Empire from Rome to Byzantium. He changed the name Byzantium to Constantinople (Istanbul). This was of major significance because it furthered division between east and west. Already east and west differed in language, with Latin spoken in the west, while Greek was spoken in the east. Although the leadership of the Bishop of Rome had been acknowledged in early Councils (which were held in the east), the role of the Bishop of Constantinople (founded in the fourth century) came to be regarded as more and more important for eastern Christians. Eventually the division became formal in 1054, when the Christian Church split into the western Church led by Rome and the eastern Orthodox Church led by Constantinople.

D. The biggest challenge to Christians in the first thousand years was the spread of Islam. Much of the Middle East, Northern Africa, Spain and Eastern Europe became Islamic.

2. The Dark Ages

On the night of 31 December 406, the Roman sentries on the River Rhine heard a terrifying sound coming through the darkness from the far bank, the sound of a vast army poised for invasion. Soon they could see the whole surface of the river covered with human forms, rafts crowded with warriors, men and horses swimming or clinging to floating tree trunks, barbaric swords and helmets glittering in the frosty air. Within minutes, the invaders were landing on the Roman side of the river and the few defenders either ran for their lives or were massacred where they stood. The days of the Roman Empire in the west were numbered.

This description in *The Christian Heritage* tells of the beginning of the barbarian invasion of Europe and the collapse of the Roman Empire. The advanced civilisation of the Roman Empire began to crumble.

Some features of Christianity at this time
A. The Church became the only institution which kept civilisation alive.
B. Some pagan peoples, for example the Irish, were converted to Christianity.
C. Monasteries were set up.
D. Congregations tended to become less active participants in the Liturgy.

3. The Middle Ages

Many people expected the world to come to an end in the year 1,000. This belief was based on the mysterious chapter 20 of the Book of Revelation, which spoke of a thousand-year reign by Christ and his saints and also of a dragon which was to be released on the world after an imprisonment of a thousand years. This belief would not have been as widespread as it was had not the state of the world been so wretched. Things were so bad, they could scarcely be worse. Europe was in a mood of despair. The year 1,000 came and went and the world did not come to an end. Hope began to revive again, encouraged by signs of a turn in the tide. The savage Hungarians received their first Christian king in 1001, the Norwegians in 1016. The ruler of Kiev, Prince Vladimir, established Christianity in Russia before his death in 1015.... Europe was now becoming a Christian continent.

The Christian Heritage

Some features of Christianity at this time
A. The Church which had protected civilisation during the Dark Ages now began to dominate every aspect of European life: art, architecture, music, education, leisure. This was the age of faith. Europe had become Christendom (the real home of Christians)

B. The Mass, which is the centre of religious life, was still said in Latin, though it was no longer the language of the people – the people became less and less involved in the liturgical rites.

c. The great Gothic cathedrals were built.

D. The orders of the friars e.g. Franciscans and Dominicans, were established.

E. Towards the end of the Middle Ages many leading Churchmen became more interested in money than in religion, leading to corruption within the Church.

4. The Renaissance and the Reformation

The Renaissance and the Reformation brought the Middle Ages to an end. Renaissance means 'rebirth' and brought a renewed interest in ancient Greek and Roman civilisation. Whereas Christian themes dominated the art, education, music and literature of the Middle Ages, the focus of the Renaissance was the human person. While people like Leonardo da Vinci and Michelangelo used many religious themes for their art, gods and goddesses of ancient Greece and Rome inspired the thought and the work of much of the Renaissance period. The Age of Faith was over. The emphasis now was on the human being.

Virgin and child with a cat, by Leonardo da Vinci.
Courtesy The British Museum.

Some characteristics of Christianity at this time

A. The Church was badly in need of reform because of abuses, e.g. nepotism, pluralism, simony, sale of indulgences.

B. The Catholic Church was split into the Catholic Church and the Protestant Churches, e.g. Lutheran, Calvinist, Presbyterian.

C. The Catholic Counter-Reformation tried to reform the Church from within. The Council of Trent dealt with doctrine and discipline – restating Church teaching on the Mass, sacraments, etc. and reforming the clergy.

The Reformation of the sixteenth century caused the second great split in Christianity. No longer was there one Christian Church in the west with Rome as its head. Now there were many Christian Churches, each with its own leader or system of rule. The divisions of Christianity are shown in this chart.

Early Christian Church 1054	
Eastern Orthodox Church (Constantinople)	Catholic Church 16th century
	Lutheran (Germany)
	Calvinist (Switzerland)
	Presbyterian (Scotland & Northern Ireland)
	Anglican (England)

Thus, today, when we speak of Christianity, we speak of those who believe in Jesus Christ as their Saviour. This belief is common to all Christians and distinguishes them from other world religions. How these Christian Churches differ will be the subject of another chapter.

SUMMARY CHART

1. Founder of Christianity – Jesus Christ	– Sources: New Testament and Other Sources – Jesus as Prophet
2. Key beliefs	– summarised in the Creed
3. The Christian Way	– Love: Two great commandments – Prayer – Our Father

4. Early Christianity	– History
	– Characteristics a. Catechumenate
	                          b. Ecclesia
	                          c. Church Fathers
	                          d. Eucharist

5. The spread of Christianity	a. The Christian Empire b. The Dark Ages c. The Middle Ages d. The Renaissance and the Reformation

Revision questions and exercises
1. The Edict of Milan (313 AD) was a turning-point for Christianity. Why?
2. Discuss the development of Christianity through the ages.

154

CHAPTER 11

The Foundations of Christian Faith

Faith, Hope and Love

This chapter discusses the foundations of Christian faith – faith, hope and love. Without the eyes of faith, without abandoning the search mentality and choosing to commit ourselves to Christ, we can never come to know what Christianity is really about. Christianity claims that Jesus Christ is Saviour, that is to say, he is the foundation of all our human hopes. He is the foundation of our hopes because in conquering death, he overcame the greatest obstacle to human hope. This total act of love is what gives us reason for hope.

Introduction– Christian Faith

In 'Christmas', the poet John Betjeman asks,

And is it true? And is it true,
  This most tremendous tale of all,
Seen in a stained-glass window's hue,
  A Baby in an ox's stall?
The maker of the stars and sea
Became a Child on earth for me?

No love that in a family dwells,
  No carolling in frosty air,
Nor all the steeple-shaking bells
  Can with this single Truth compare –
That God was Man in Palestine
And lives to-day in Bread and Wine.

In this poem Betjeman captures what is unique about Christianity. For nearly two thousand years, millions of Christians all over the world have claimed that God becoming human in Jesus Christ is the single most important event, not just for the world, but for our understanding of God and of ourselves.

- Does this claim stand up?
- Does this truth mean anything to us as we try to live and find happiness in the world?
- Does Jesus Christ make any difference to my life?

The Eyes of Faith

'God was Man in Palestine' expresses a core belief of Christian faith. However, we are still left with the question, 'And is it true, this most tremendous tale of all?'

To answer this question demands a certain attitude of mind. Firstly, it demands that we are open to the experience of mystery in life – to that aspect of life that may not be immediately obvious – to that aspect of life that is most accessible through imagination, poetry and love, which sense that 'the beauty of the world, the great works of art, the warmth of love can [not] arise from the mere combination of atoms' (*The Inner Truth*, Bishop Donal Murray).

Questions and exercises
1. How can people be closed to the sense of mystery in life?
2. What is meant by the statement 'there are different forms of truth'?
3. Describe beauty – how difficult an exercise do you find this?

Secondly, to believe in Jesus Christ, we must abandon the search mentality we adopted in looking at ways to God. We must also abandon the objective stance we took when looking at world religions. Christian faith is an inside job. Ultimately, each one of us must decide whether or not Jesus Christ is God's personal revelation to us, and the fulfilment of all our hopes and aspirations. It is not something that anyone else can do for us. It is our choice.

> Either this man was the human face of God or else millions have based their lives on an illusion. My unbelieving friends might not accept that stark either true-or-false. They might regard the historical figure of Jesus as a great religious leader, a spiritual genius, someone who embodies the hopes of humanity to live with love. They might see his story as a poem of visionary inspiration. They might reverence his life and death as they would that of Gandhi or Martin Luther King. But without crossing the threshold into faith, they cannot reach what is central to the vision of Jesus in the gospels – a relationship with God as his Father and a conviction that he came from God to inaugurate a new way of living called the Kingdom.
>
> *Free to Believe*, Michael Paul Gallagher

An old Polish Jew who survived the massacre of the Warsaw ghetto said:
> As I looked at that man upon the cross.... I knew I must make up my mind once and for all, and either take my stand beside him and share in his undefeated faith in God.... or else fall finally into a bottomless pit of bitterness, hatred and unutterable despair.

In many ways this is the most difficult step of all to take. We can see this most clearly if we compare 'crossing the threshold into faith' with getting married. Consider all the romantic books ever written or films ever made. There is something very attractive about the chase and the novelty of a relationship before marriage. The very uncertainty seems to make the relationship more exciting. Marriage by comparison seems, at least to the outsider, to lose that sense of magic, to become more predictable and therefore more mundane. Marriage makes demands. It is often only those who have made such a commitment who can experience and understand the new security and freedom which marriage can bring.

And so it is with Christian faith. Deciding to commit ourselves to Christ may cost too much. It is easy to reverence from afar. The demands which Christian faith makes may seem too much. Yet, as with the commitment of marriage, we can only know the freedom and joy which Christ brings by taking that step into faith ourselves.

Questions
1. Why do people find it difficult to commit themselves to something?
2. Examine the commitments in your own life. How do they benefit you?

Indeed, any interest which is expressed in Jesus Christ is directly related to Christian faith. Few are interested in Jesus simply as they would be in Napoleon or Hitler. This obscure prophet from Nazareth is only significant because of the effect which he has had on people and on the world, as this description shows:
> Here is a man,
> the child of a peasant woman..
> He never wrote a book.
> He never held an office.
> He never owned a home.
> He never had a family.
> He never went to college.
> He never put a foot inside a big city.
> He never travelled two hundred miles from the place where he was born.
> He never did one of the things that usually accompany greatness.
> He had no credentials but himself....
> While still a young man the tide of popular opinion turned against him.
> His friends ran away.
> One of them denied him.
> He was turned over to his enemies.

He went through the mockery of a trial.

He was nailed to a cross between two thieves.

His executioners gambled for the only piece of property he had on earth .... his coat.

When he was dead he was taken down and laid in a borrowed grave through the pity of
 a friend.

Nineteen wide centuries have come and gone and he is still the centrepiece of the
human race and the leader of the column of progress.

I am far within the mark when I say that

all the armies that ever marched

all the navies that were ever built

all the parliaments that ever sat

and all the kings that ever reigned

put together

have not affected the life of man

upon earth as powerfully as that

One Solitary Life.

Author unknown

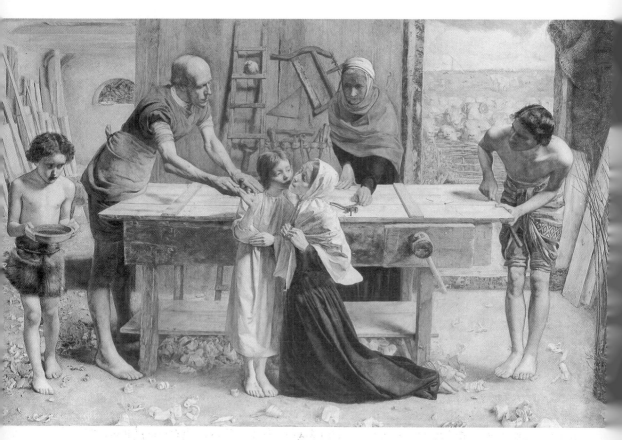

Christ in the House of his Parents, by Millais. *Courtesy The Tate Gallery, London.*

Questions
1. What impresses you most about the life of Jesus?
2. Is it true to say that 'all the armies that ever marched.... have not affected the life of man upon earth as powerfully as that one solitary life'?

People are only interested in Jesus Christ because Christianity – the expression of belief in Jesus Christ – has persisted down through the centuries. The main source of our information on Jesus Christ – the New Testament – is itself a testimony of faith, written by those who believed so that others might believe.

> The New Testament writings are only there because Jesus received a faith beyond his death, and because the first believers collected together, handed on and finally set down in writing, the reports on Jesus, for the needs of their communities: for their liturgy, their religious instruction, and for missionary preaching, and to introduce order into their churches... If it were not for that interest we would know as little about Jesus of Nazareth as about other itinerant preachers of his time.
>
> *Jesus the Christ*, Walter Kasper

Therefore, it is only in and through the very faith of the apostles and the early Church that we can know about Jesus of Nazareth at all. Indeed, we ourselves can only come to Christian faith because we experience it as lived, proclaimed and practised in the Christian Churches. In this sense we differ from the first Christians. They knew the person of Jesus – his life, his words and his deeds – and so came to believe in him. We begin with the experience of Christianity and only then do we go back to discover the person of Jesus Christ.

So, as we begin our study of Christian faith, our question is not so much 'How do we prove the claims and the promises of Jesus Christ?', but, rather, 'What does the life, death and resurrection of Jesus Christ mean for our understanding of ourselves and our world?'

Questions
1. Do you think that it is a help or a hindrance to your faith that you have been born into Christianity?
2. One writer makes the charge that 'the reality of Christ, his person, has been manipulated, distorted, commandeered, "kidnapped".' Do you agree? Explain.
2. What is your image of Jesus?

Messianic hope

Christianity claims that Jesus Christ is the saviour. The language of 'saviour', 'salvation', 'redemption' may sound remote to us today, but it was *the* question at the time of Jesus. We have already seen that the Jews longed for a saviour – someone who would free them and bring about a Kingdom of justice and peace. During the season of Advent, Christians recall this great longing of the Jews for the coming of the Messiah. The first reading of each Mass during the four Sundays of Advent is taken from the Prophets who foretell the coming of a Saviour who will bring about a new kingdom.

Indeed, even in the pagan world of that time there was the hope that such a kingdom would come to be. It may be difficult for us to understand how such a desire grips a whole people, yet when we look at Northern Ireland, at South Africa, at Eastern Europe in the late 1980s, we can see how, even on a purely political level, the longing for peace and freedom can permeate a nation and, indeed, spread to many nations.

Exercises
1. Describe the mood of the country during World Cup matches.
2. Give other examples of a mood gripping a nation.

The coming of Jesus and the belief that he was the redeemer and liberator sent by God could be understood as a direct answer to the question of the age. The question, 'Are you he who is to come, or shall we look for another?' (Mt 11:13) was to be heard everywhere.

Jesus the Christ, Walter Kasper

Group Work
Look up the Old Testament readings for Advent:
Is 2:1-5; Is 11:1-10; Is 35:1-6; Is 7:10-14; Is 33:14-16; Is 40:1-5, 9-14; Jer 33:14-16; Zeph 3:14-18; 2 Sam 7:1-5, 8-11
Examine the theme of hope in these readings. What are the people hoping for?

The words of the Christmas carol, 'When a Child is Born', capture something of the messianic hope that was the Jewish experience.

A ray of hope flickers in the sky,
A tiny star lights up way up high.
All across the land, dawns a brand new morn,
This comes to pass
when a child is born.

A rosy hue settles all around
You've got the feel you're on solid ground,
For a spell or two, no-one seems forlorn,
This comes to pass when a child is born.

And all of this happens
because the world is waiting
Waiting for a child, black, white, yellow,
No one knows.
But a child who will grow up and turn tears to laughter, hate to love and war to
peace and everyone to everyone's neighbour,
and misery and suffering, will be words to be forgotten, forever.

It's all a dream, an illusion now,
It must come true, sometime soon, somehow,
All across the land, dawns a brand new morn,
This comes to pass,
when a child is born.

The real question for us today is: DO WE STILL NEED A SAVIOUR, A REDEEMER?
Do people of the twentieth century still long for, still hope for someone who will bring
peace and joy? Or even if they still long for this do they believe in other messiahs – science,
technology and political systems? Do they despair, believing life to be essentially meaningless, or is it possible for people to believe in Jesus Christ as their Messiah?

Group Work
1. Select a number of current newspapers.
2. List the 'good news' stories.
3. List the 'bad news' stories.
4. What possible solutions, if any, do you see to the 'bad news' stories?

Do we still need a Saviour?

Looking at any daily newspaper, it is clear that the world is beset by problems – war, famine,
unemployment, violence, crime. The list is depressingly endless.
Many attempts have been made to find solutions to such problems – Government pro-
grammes to try to tackle poverty and unemployment; organisations like the League of
Nations and the United Nations which have sought to promote world peace. Our history
books are full of stories of emancipation (freedom) – the liberation of the peasants/serfs, the
liberation of Jews, of blacks, of women and of colonised peoples. All sorts of political systems from democracy to communism have aimed at providing people with the means for
happiness and earthly salvation. However, as one writer notes:
> ... the brave new world has not come. Communism is not the only god that has failed.
> Feuerbach's ideas helped to shape Nietzsche who assured us that the Christian concept of
> God is sick, corrupt, the contradiction of life! Nietzsche's own ideas flowed into Adolf
> Hitler's National Socialism, a thoroughly sick, corrupt and life-destructive system if ever
> there was one.
>
> Gerald O'Collins, *The Furrow*, April 1990

Questions
1. Do you agree that 'the brave new world has not come'?
Why? Why not?

It is not that the world is no longer beset with problems and promises of solutions. On the Statue of Liberty in New York harbour, we read Emma Lazarus' words:

> Give me your tired, your poor, your huddled masses yearning to be free. The wretched refuse of your teeming shore. Send these, the homeless, tempest-tost to me, I lift my lamp beside the golden door.

It is rather that the problems and their solutions, the hopes and their fulfilment are more complex than many realised. People are more than just workers or pleasure-seekers. What all the human solutions to these problems had in common was that they understood human beings and their needs in terms of the visible world only. Ultimate or religious questions were discarded and politics, economics, science and technology were seen as answers to the questions of the age. Have we become happier and freer because philosophers like Feuerbach encouraged us to forget about the 'God solution' and get on with building a better society? Or has the absence of a spiritual or religious sense made our problems even more difficult to cope with? Carl Jung observed that 'it was not religion but its absence that caused neuroses.... He discovered that the common problem with all his patients over the age of thirty-five was finding a religious attitude to life.'

Gerald O'Collins, *The Furrow*, April 1990

Questions
1. What is the 'American dream'?
2. Has the 'American dream' come true for everyone?

Consider the following:

1. 'Man now realises that he is an accident, that he is a completely futile being, that he has to play out the game without reason.... Man can only attempt to beguile himself for a time, by prolonging his life – by buying a kind of immortality through the doctors.'

Francis Bacon – 1561-1626

2.

Imagine there's no heaven, it's easy if you try
No hell below us, above us only sky.
Imagine all the people, living for today.
Imagine there's no country, it isn't hard to do.
Nothing to kill or die for and no religion too.
Imagine all the people living life in peace

You may say that I'm a dreamer,
but I'm not the only one,
I hope some say that you'll join us
and the world will be as one.

Imagine no possessions, I wonder if you can?
No need for greed or hunger, a
brotherhood of man.
Imagine all the people sharing all the world.
You may say that I'm a dreamer
but I'm not the only one,
I hope some day you'll join us and
the world will live as one.

'Imagine' – John Lennon

3.

Be not afraid, I go before you always
Come follow me, and I will give you rest.

You shall cross the barren desert, but you
shall not die of thirst
You shall wander far in safety though
you do not know the way
You shall speak your words to foreign men
and they will understand.
You shall see the face of God and live.

If you pass through raging waters,
in the sea you shall not drown.
If you walk amid the burning flames
you shall not be harmed,
If you stand before the power of hell and
death is at your side
You shall see the face of God and live.

Blessed are your poor,
for the kingdom shall be theirs
Blessed are you who weep and mourn
for one day you shall laugh.
And if wicked men insult and hate
you all because of me,
Blessed, blessed are you.
(Based on Isaiah 43:1-5 and Lk 6:20-23)

Questions
1. What attitude to life is communicated in each of these quotations/songs?
2. Which of the above best describes your own attitude to life?
3. Which do you find most hopeful?

Human hope

Most of the time, we refuse to despair. Even when the odds are stacked against us, we continue to hope against hope.

The life of cerebral palsy victim Christy Brown inspired the Oscar-winning film, *My Left Foot*. Christy was the son of a Dublin bricklayer and was born so severely crippled by cerebral palsy that the doctors wrote him off as severely mentally handicapped. For many people, the real heroine in the story is Christy's mother. Despite poverty, and having to look after her other children, she always made personal time for Christy. Even when all the evidence seemed against it, she persisted with the belief that there was much more to Christy. Finally it was proved that he was something of a genius. With his mother's unwavering belief in him, he painted countless pictures with his left foot and went on to write five books.

On 4 January 1994 a Cork teenager, Carrie Grandon, lost her fight for life. She suffered from cystic fibrosis and had been on a waiting-list for a heart and lung transplant at Great Ormond Street Children's Hospital in London since 1991.

She was almost fourteen years old and her school friends were planning a surprise party for her. A month before she died she had written a letter to newspapers explaining that without the transplant she would die.

Her mother was interviewed on RTE Radio on the day she died. While she was, understandably, heartbroken, she paid a warm tribute to all those who had cared for Carrie and announced that someone else would get the gift of sight because the family had donated Carrie's eyes. Here were a sadness and a loss tinged with hope and generosity.

Considering these two stories and, indeed, the many stories of hope which we know of, we are reminded of the words of St Paul:

> We are afflicted in every way
> but not crushed; perplexed but
> not driven to despair; persecuted
> but not forsaken; struck down
> but not destroyed; (2 Cor 4:8-9)

Questions
1. Why do you think that Christy's mother and Carrie's mother continued to hope despite the odds?
2. Give other examples of people continuing to 'hope against hope'.

Christian hope

What lies behind and gives reason for human hope? What does Christian hope have to offer to human hope? What sustains St Paul's belief?

Question
How would you answer these questions?

To believe that things will turn out as you anticipate is not hope, but optimism.... The virtue of hope does not mean expecting that particular events will turn out in a particular way. It means recognising that the entire universe, and its history, is in the hands of God who is leading it to himself (*Jesus is Lord*, Bishop Donal Murray).

Question
What is the difference between hope and optimism?

Behind the refusal to despair lies the hope that ultimately everything will be all right. In his book *A Rumour of Angels*, Peter Berger makes the following observations:

A child wakes up in the night, perhaps from a bad dream, and finds himself surrounded by darkness, alone, beset by nameless threats. At such a moment… the child cries out for his mother… she will turn on a lamp, perhaps, which will encircle the scene with a warm glow of reassuring light. She will speak or sing to the child…. 'Don't be afraid – everything is all right.' If all goes well, the child will be reassured, and in his trust he will return to sleep.

Berger goes on to ask the question – 'Is the mother lying to the child? Will everything be all right?' He concludes that ultimately this is a religious hope that indeed everything will be all right – that the world will not descend into chaos – that life – my life, the child's life, has ultimate meaning. This is the hope expressed by the Psalmist:

The Lord is my shepherd, I shall not want;
he makes me lie down in green pastures;
He leads me beside still waters; he restores my soul.
He leads me in paths of righteousness for his name's sake. Even though I walk
through the valley of the shadow of death, I fear no evil; for thou art with me;
thy rod and thy staff, they comfort me. (Ps 23: 1-4)

It is not a hope, however, that denies evil and suffering. It is a hope 'even though…' there is much misery. Suffering and evil will continue to exist but they do not swamp us.

Neither is it a list of things we imagine would make us happy, for hope does not mean expecting things to work out in particular ways.

There is a difference between our hopes, namely the things we hope for, and hope. Hope goes deeper than all of these things..... 'The hoper, and he alone, anticipates nothing; he holds himself in readiness for a fulfilment still to come, although he is aware that he knows neither its dimensions nor its time (*Jesus is Lord*).

The one who hopes in this way is sustained by the belief that 'there is indeed something or someone at the heart of the universe that makes it trustworthy and renders the world and human existence meaningful. This something or someone is usually called "God"' (*What is God*, J. F. Haught).

Questions and exercise
1. Reflect on the statement that 'there is indeed something or someone at the heart of the universe that makes it trustworthy and renders the world and human existence meaningful'.
2. What does this statement mean?
3. How does it make you feel?

Love: The foundation of Christian hope

If the kind of hope we have been talking about is more than just an illusion or mere wishful thinking, it must be founded on something solid. If hope is to mean anything, it must survive disappointments and setbacks. Ultimately, it must survive death. For the Christian, Jesus Christ is the foundation of hope. He is the foundation of our hope because he revealed God's absolute and unconditional love for his people. Through his life, death and resurrection, he demonstrated that God never forgets or abandons his creatures. By accepting death on the Cross, by not counting death too high a price to pay for love, he enabled love to triumph over the ultimate threat to human hope, namely death.

> I am the Good Shepherd who is willing to die for the sheep. When the hired man who is not a shepherd and does not own the sheep, sees a wolf coming, he leaves the sheep and runs away; so the wolf snatches the sheep and scatters them. The hired man runs away and does not care about the sheep. I am the Good Shepherd. As the Father knows me and I know the Father, in the same way, I know my sheep and they know me. And I am willing to die for them. (Jn 10:11-15)

Death has been conquered by extreme love. This is the foundation of our hope. the human things that reassure us and give us confidence – our families and friends, our money, our jobs – are only temporary sources of hope and strength for us. They are only temporary because they too will pass away. Human truth, justice, friendship and even the kind of love expressed by people like Christy Brown's mother and Mrs Grandon are the experiences which enable us to hope, but they need an ultimate foundation or they too will pass away. The Christian believes that despite suffering and death, there is still every reason to hope and to live with joy, for:

God works with those who love him. those who have been called in accordance with his purpose, and turns everything to their good. (Rom 8:28)

This is why:

No love that in a family dwells,
No carolling in frosty air,
Nor all the steeple-shaking bells
Can with this single Truth compare –
That God was Man in Palestine.
And lives to-day in Bread and Wine.'
('Christmas', John Betjeman)

Adoration of the Magi

SUMMARY CHART

1. Faith	a. The eyes of faith b. 'An inside job' – we cannot believe without becoming involved. c. Faith in Jesus as witnessed by the New Testament and the Church
2. Hope	a. Messianic hope b. Do we still need a Saviour? c. Human hope d. Christian hope – the foundation of human hope
3. Love	The foundation of Christian hope is love, because through Jesus Christ, death has been conquered.

Revision questions and exercises
1. What is meant by the 'eyes of faith'?
2. Why may 'deciding to abandon the search and commit oneself to Christ' cost too much?
3. Why do people hope?
4. If you were asked, 'What difference does Christianity make to life?', what answer would you give?

CHAPTER 12

The Challenge of Christian Faith

This chapter begins by acknowledging that the real problem facing Christianity is not atheism but apathy or indifference. It suggests that this experience of indifference is rooted in the sense of the superficial. The challenge of Christianity is to resist the superficial and so be free to live life more deeply and more freely. This challenge involves a radical change of heart on our part and a call to live in the world in a very different way.

Introduction: The Experience of Indifference

A teacher in a post-primary school in Ireland once showed a Leaving Certificate class a video on non-belief. The programme featured a number of people who had abandoned their faith and now described themselves as humanists. They went on to explain how they find meaning and fulfilment in life without reference to religion and without belief in a God or an afterlife. In all cases the individuals had thought seriously about religion and its role in their lives. For a variety of reasons, each one had decided that atheism or agnosticism was a more honest step for them to take. To have continued with religious practice without personally believing seemed hypocritical to them.

Having watched the video, the students were asked whether or not they would be attracted to atheism, agnosticism, or humanism, as it was described. Their answers proved very interesting. While not one student was attracted to such a thought-out path of unbelief, the reasons given for this were: 'laziness', 'I couldn't be bothered,' 'It doesn't make any difference to my life.'

Question
Can you identify with the responses given by this Leaving Certificate class? Explain.

These answers suggest that many people continue to believe or, perhaps more accurately, do not become fully-fledged non-believers, not as a result of any conscious decision about faith, but rather out of a sense of apathy or indifference towards the whole question of religious faith. They continue to 'believe', but faith is more a non-decision than a true option and commitment. The result is a kind of 'practical unbelief' where, as St Paul describes it, a person holds the form of religion but denies the power of it (2 Tm 3:5).

> In this light 'practical unbelief' means that the truth revealed in Christ remains simply unreal, unrecognised and unlived, and this vague situation of non-involvement is now more frequent than the older atheism of an intellectual or political rejection of God. *What will give us happiness?* Cardinal Paul Poupard & Michael Paul Gallagher

The Origins of Indifference

Soren Kierkegaard

'This vague situation of non-involvement' or indifference towards faith has its origins in our experience of the modern world. The nineteenth-century Danish philosopher, Soren Kierkegaard, interpreted this modern experience as follows:

> Let others moan about this evil age. I complain about its meanness, its lack of passion. Life is reduced to one colour.

'Life is reduced to one colour.' There is a sense in which we can identify with this statement. Consider how much of life we regard as boring, everyday and routine. When we look back on any length of time, the days seem to blend together. We have drifted through them sometimes like lifeless forms carried by a tide. There often seems to be very little colour, excitement or life in our days.

Mostly, we are undisturbed by such a lack of life or enthusiasm. Indeed, we may feel that it is a more desirable state of being than that of pain or suffering which would wake us from our slumber. Sometimes we may feel that we are missing out on something, but we usually end up settling for a secondary kind of happiness which may not be earth-moving but which makes few demands on us.

Concerned as we may be with coping with the present and providing whatever immediate comforts we may seek, we deaden ourselves to some of the bigger questions and hungers that have always been part of the human experience. Closed as we are to a depth dimension in our life and in our experience it is no wonder that

> some never get to the point of raising questions about God, since they seem to experience no religious stirrings nor do they sense why they should trouble themselves about religion (*Gaudium et spes* 19).

? Question
Do you agree with what Vatican II is saying here? Explain.

The Challenge to Awaken

Earlier we observed the lament of a middle-aged housewife about her unused life as portrayed in the film *Shirley Valentine*.

> I've led such a little life and even that'll be over pretty soon. I've allowed myself to lead this little life when inside me there's so much more and it's all gone unused and now it will never be used. Why do we get all this life if we don't ever use it? Why do we get all these feelings and dreams and hopes if we don't ever use them? That's where Shirley Valentine disappeared to – she got lost in all this unused life.

Here is somebody who has been caught up in the routine of life described earlier. As wife and mother she had done the normal things that any wife and mother does. But now she is uneasy, restless and disturbed. Looking back on her life she feels a certain sense of dissatisfaction. There is disappointment at the realisation that she somehow 'got lost in all this unused life'. She has so many feelings, dreams and hopes deep within her that she has allowed to remain dormant. She has settled for secondary fulfilment but now she craves something more – but what price, this 'something more'?

In T.S. Eliot's poem, 'The Love Song of J. Alfred Prufrock', the drama between primary and secondary calls is played out in the life of one individual.

The superficial self is preoccupied with routine:

> *There will be time, there will be time*
> *To prepare a face to meet the faces that you meet;*
>
> *My morning coat, my collar mounting firmly to the chin,*
> *My necktie rich and modest, but asserted by a simple pin –*
>
> *I shall wear the bottom of my trousers rolled.*
>
> *I have measured out my life with coffee spoons;*
>
> *In the room the women come and go*
> *Talking of Michelangelo.*

Then the deeper self tries to emerge:

> *Do I dare*
> *Disturb the universe?*
> *Should I, after tea and cakes and ices,*
> *Have the strength to force the moment to its crisis?*
>
> *Would it have been worth while*
> *To have bitten off the matter with a smile,*

To have squeezed the universe into a ball
To roll it toward some overwhelming question,

I have seen the moment of my greatness flicker...

Here Prufrock is torn between two selves and two lives – the superficial self which is concerned with a life of calm, deliberate, detached normality and order as represented in his experience of high society life, his attempt to put on a show for those he will meet and his preoccupation with appearances – his morning coat, his necktie 'rich and modest', his partaking of 'tea and cakes and ices'.

But he has glimpsed something better. A door has been opened slightly and he is caught in a dilemma. Should he seize the moment and taste the excitement of what he has glimpsed? Should he pass through the open door and explore or should he remain where he is? 'Would it have been worth while?' He is attracted, yet reluctant, all the while realising that he is missing something: I have seen the moment of my greatness flicker.

In Shirley Valentine's lament and Prufrock's dilemma we glimpse the tension between the desire to live more fully and the temptation back into a more routine and superficial existence.
If we examine our own lives, we may find that much of our existence is at a superficial level. Indeed, it is probably true to say that some people go through their entire lives without being prompted by the questions and struggles we have just observed. Yet, few people avoid the experience either of love or of suffering – the great awareness of something deeper in us.

> Whenever a person runs into love, the heart awakens from the superficial, but even more infallibly, whenever a person runs into tragedy and manages to find courage to respond with wisdom, the door is open to a different dimension of happiness.
> *What will give us Happiness?* Cardinal Paul Poupard and Michael Paul Gallagher

Exercise
Reflect on the experiences in your own life which seem to awaken you.
How did such experiences make you feel?

Consider how we feel at such moments. However short-lived these moments are in our lives, they make us feel uplifted, vibrant and alive. The very experience of love frees us and draws us out of ourselves towards the other. Love challenges us beyond the superficial to a deeper experience of living. It awakens in us some of those 'feelings, dreams and hopes' already mentioned. It makes us feel that we are called to something bigger and better. At such times, the Greek writer Nikos Kazantzakis' picture of God as a Great Cry which echoes inside every being, urging it onwards and upwards may make sense to us.

> Blowing through heaven and earth, and in our hearts and the heart of every living thing, is a gigantic breath – a Great Cry – which we call God. Plant life wished to continue its motionless sleep next to stagnant waters, but the Cry leaped up within it and violently shook its roots; 'Away, let go of the earth, walk!' Had the tree been able to think and

judge, it would have cried, 'I don't want to. What are you urging me to do? You are demanding the impossible!' But the Cry, without pity, kept shaking its roots and shouting, 'Away, let go of the earth, walk!' It shouted in this way for thousands of eons; and lo! as a result of desire and struggle, life escaped the motionless tree and was liberated.

Animals appeared – worms – making themselves at home in water and mud. 'We're just fine here,' they said, 'We have peace and security; we're not budging!'

But the terrible Cry hammered itself pitilessly into their loins.

'Leave the mud, stand up; give birth to your betters!'

'We don't want to! We can't!'

'You can't, but I can. Stand up!'

And lo! after thousands of eons, man emerged trembling on his still unsolid legs.

The human being is a centaur; his equine hooves are planted in the ground, but his body from breast to head is worked on and tormented by the merciless Cry. He has been fighting, again for thousands of eons, to draw himself, like a sword, out of his animalistic scabbard. He is also fighting – this is his new struggle – to draw himself out of his human scabbard. Man calls in despair, 'Where can I go? I have reached the pinnacle, beyond is the abyss.' And the Cry answers, 'I am beyond. Stand up!'

The challenge to be free

The key idea running through everything we have been talking about so far is that there are, in a sense, two sides to human nature – an everyday, somewhat superficial side masks a deeper and more authentic side. While we may be prompted out of our superficial existence by the experience of either love or suffering it is a struggle to live and remain at a deeper level. The temptations back into superficial living – laziness, comfort and materialism – can sometimes prove too alluring. The struggle to be free from such temptations is an ongoing one.

In the film *Saving Grace*, Tom Conti plays a Pope who leaves the Vatican and goes to work in the poor village of Montepedro. In this village he finds an utterly dispirited people. They have engineered an 'epidemic' so that they will receive free food. So low is their morale that they make no effort whatsoever to improve their situation. The irrigation scheme which would have helped to grow food has fallen into disrepair but no one makes any effort to fix it. Indeed, when any attempt is made, it is quickly stopped by the so-called village leaders who want things to remain as they are. So hopeless does their situation seem that they see no reason for trying to rise above it. Unaware of his identity, they are quite hostile when the Pope tries to get the irrigation scheme going to enable them to live a better life. It takes much effort and the death of a boy to free the people from the situation to which they have become enslaved. At the end of the film the main characters in the village are changed people. They have been lifted out of their old and destructive selves. They have been set free.

Question
1. What understanding of freedom is presented to us here?
2. Why do you think people resist this freedom?

The call to be free, which is a key call in Christianity, is all too often difficult to respond to. In the story of the Grand Inquisitor (*The Brothers Karamazov*), Dostoyevsky presents a powerful reflection on human resistance to freedom.

The story is set in the sixteenth century in Seville at the time of the Spanish Inquisition. Fifteen hundred years after his first appearance on earth, Jesus visits once again and encounters the person of the Grand Inquisitor, who immediately challenges him:

> Why then did you come to meddle with us?

The Grand Inquisitor goes on to explain what he means by 'meddle'.
When Jesus was first on earth he called on people to believe in his path to happiness – the path of freedom – freedom from the false promises of happiness which the world presented. However, it was to be people's own choice whether they would accept this call or not:

> their freedom of faith was dearer
> to you than anything even
> in those days, fifteen hundred years ago.
> You wanted man's free love so that he would follow you fully, fascinated and captivated by you.

Fifteen hundred years later, the Grand Inquisitor argues, it is obvious that people could not cope with this freedom. It was too much of a burden for them, too great a challenge. So they settled for less. This could have been anticipated, for Jesus himself was tempted out of a life of freedom.

> the great spirit talked with you in the wilderness and we are told in the books that he
> apparently 'tempted' you.

With promises of bread, power and pride 'the whole future history of mankind' is anticipated.

 Exercise
Examine the temptations of Christ as presented in Matthew 4:1-11.

Just as Jesus was tempted to turn the stones into bread to make people believe in him, just as he was tempted to worship Satan by being promised power over the kingdoms of the earth and just as he was tempted to test the power of God by throwing himself off a high temple, so too we are tempted. Such temptations provide for immediate satisfaction. How many people crave 'bread', material possessions or any other fulfilments of the hunger of the body? How many people crave success and power and how many people trust so much in their own resources and abilities so as to render surrender to God impossible?
This is, therefore, the first main struggle and challenge which Christianity presents to us – to live deeply and in freedom, to seek true happiness and to recognise that this is impossible on our own. We often miss the mark. This is essentially what sin is – a failure to live up to what we can truly be. We cannot conquer this false self alone or by our own efforts. As Bishop Walter Kasper puts it:

Man cannot free himself by his own power. He cannot pull himself out of the swamp by his own bootlaces.
Jesus the Christ

The New Testament presents Jesus as the saviour, the liberator who forgives our sins and frees us to be fully human.

The Challenge of the World

When we look at today's world, we can identify a number of attitudes towards the world and its people. There still is, as there has always been, a selfish and self-seeking mentality where our own happiness is our only concern. This kind of mentality can be described as *individualism* and it was explained in the following way by the French philosopher Alexis de Tocqueville when he visited America in the 1830s.

> Individualism is a calm and considered feeling which disposes each citizen to isolate himself from the mass of his fellows and withdraw into the circle of family and friends; with this eclectic society formed to his taste, he gladly leaves the greater society to look after itself. There are more and more people who, though neither rich nor powerful enough to have much hold over others, have gained or kept enough wealth and enough understanding to look after their own needs. Such folk owe no man anything and hardly expect anything from anybody. They form the habit of thinking of themselves in isolation and imagine that their whole destiny is in their hands.
>
> *Democracy in America*, A. de Tocqueville

The people described here do not appear to be bad. They rarely do direct harm to anyone else. They rarely break the law. They do not rely on the State or ask for much from other people. They are largely self-sufficient. They look after their own needs and those of their immediate family and friends. They have no need to depend on others.

However, they are often too wrapped up in themselves to be generous or concerned about the people outside their world. Indeed, sometimes, instead of helping others less fortunate than they are, they are critical of such people. Behind such criticism lies some of the following thoughts: 'If I can make a go of my life, why shouldn't others .... let everyone fend for him or herself .... I mind my own business, let other people mind theirs.'

Another group of people have a different set of priorities. We know them as the 'Mother Teresas' of history whom the world admires. We know them too in the less famous, the less obvious people who quietly live their lives for others and whose kindness and generosity can sometimes go unnoticed. Again, such people have always existed – but as we approach the end of the twentieth century we can sense a new spirit of care about the world, its people and their problems. The dangers posed to the environment by industrialisation, the human and material cost of war and armaments and the sight of starving children brought into our living-rooms by television have begun to alert us to the fact that it is not good enough to concern ourselves with our exclusive needs alone.

At the very minimum, we are beginning to realise that what we do today to the environment will have repercussions for our children. The instant TV pictures of the horrors of war and famine move even the indifferent at least to question, if not act upon, such waste.

In an address given to the United Nations, the former Soviet President, Mikhail Gorbachev, shared this realisation:

> On the whole our credo is ... human problems can be resolved only in a human way ... the concept of development at another's expense is becoming impossible if it disregards human and national rights and freedoms or is detrimental to the environment.

To people so moved, the words of Mikhail Gorbachev, unthinkable from previous Soviet presidents, seem inspiring and very human. They are words of salvation – solutions to the world's problems. All over the world we find people and organisations calling for civil rights and disarmament. We find groups concerned with protecting the environment while others dedicate themselves to feeding the hungry. Such concern is deeply human and rightly wins the admiration of decent-minded people. Our question here is, Where does Christianity stand within this scenario? We know that human concern is not unique to Christianity. Yet the challenge of Christianity is specific.

The Kingdom of God

The central message of Christianity is the coming of the Kingdom of God. Our understanding of what is meant by the Kingdom of God may be impeded by our modern understanding of kingdom. To us, the notion of kingdom probably conjures up images like authority, rule, law and order – a certain inequality, a certain limiting of people's freedom.

> In the ancient world it was completely the opposite. For the Jews of Jesus' time the kingdom of God was the essence of the hope for the establishment of a just ruler which was never fulfilled on earth. In that ancient Middle Eastern conception, Justice did not consist primarily in impartial judgements, but in help and protection for the helpless, weak and poor. The coming of the kingdom of God was expected to be liberation from unjust rule and the establishment of the justice of God in the world. The kingdom of God was the main element of the hope for salvation.
>
> *Jesus, the Christ*, Walter Kasper

The theme running through the whole Bible is that human begins are incapable of possessing or providing peace, justice and freedom by their own efforts alone. The history of humankind has shown that peace is constantly threatened, justice is violated and freedom is suppressed. Therefore, from the biblical point of view, what is needed is a completely new start which God alone can provide. This new start is what is meant by the kingdom of God.

Jesus and the Kingdom of God

Jesus came to a people who already believed that God was personally active in their history. He came to a people who expected a new start, who expected that the Kingdom of God would be established, albeit in different ways. The Zealots, for instance, believed that the Kingdom of God would be brought about by a political uprising and the use of force.

The Pharisees believed that the Kingdom of God would be brought about by observing the law. Jesus himself never defined the Kingdom. Rather, in announcing that the Kingdom of God was at hand, he at the same time called on people to repent and believe in the Good News.

> The time is fulfilled, and the kingdom of God is at hand;
> repent and believe in the Gospel. (Mk 1:15)

Implicit in this is the invitation to a new and different kind of living, which would build a new world. In this sense the message of Jesus Christ challenges the priorities of the world and turns them upside down. It calls for a radical change of heart from those who accept the Christian way. The Welsh poet, R.S. Thomas, describes it thus:

> It's a long way but inside it
> There are quite different things going on:
> Festivals at which the poor man
> Is king and the consumptive is
> Healed; mirrors in which the blind look
> At themselves and love looks at them
> Back; and industry is for mending
> The bent bones and the minds fractured
> by life. It's a long way off, but to get
> There takes no time and admission
> Is free, if you purge yourself
> Of desire, and present yourself with
> Your need only and the simple offering
> Of your faith, green as a leaf.
> 'The Kingdom'

The World Says:	Jesus says:	
Money, success, power, these are what count. Happiness is – high living.	Blessed are the poor in spirit, for theirs is the kingdom of God.	– Don't have an exaggerated sense of your own importance. – Don't try to go it alone in life. – Foster a non-possessive attitude towards life and people. – Know your need of God.
Be tough Don't let anything get to you. Don't get involved in other people's problems.	Blessed are those who mourn, for they shall be comforted.	– Allow yourself to be touched by the pain of others. – Feel deeply, care, no matter what it costs you in time and emotion. 'Weep with those who weep'.
Trample – rather than be trampled on. Get ahead at all costs. Always assert your rights. 'No one will get the upper hand while you're around'.	Blessed are the gentle, for they shall inherit the earth.	– Respond to situations, don't just react. – From your inner strength in God, try to overcome evil by good. – sensitivity is not weakness.
'I'm all right Jack!' So long as the problem doesn't affect me, or my pocket, I don't care. 'What's in it for me?'	Blessed are those who hunger and thirst for righteousness, they shall be satisfied.	– Have a sense of integrity. – 'Be not dismayed at finding wrong, but do your best to put it right.' – See that justice and fair play are the rules of the game.
Never admit to being wrong yourself, and take a tough stand with anyone who falls short.	Blessed are the merciful, for they shall obtain mercy.	– Don't cast the first stone. – Don't kick someone who's down. – Make allowances. You don't know the whole story. – Remember, you are grateful for understanding when you are in the wrong yourself.
Be casual in your approach to life and love. Deal in 'double meanings'. Trivalise what's important. If you take life seriously, it will make demands on you.	Blessed are the pure in heart, for they shall see God.	– Have at heart the things of God. – Really care about people – yourself and others. – Let people feel 'special' and of value when they are in contact with you.
Operate on the basis of 'an eye for an eye and a tooth for a tooth'. Hold grudges and resentments. Be a trouble-maker, throw your weight around.	Blessed are the peacemakers, for they shall be called children of God.	– Be at peace within yourself and radiate this to others. – Specialise in healing rifts at home/school/work... – Be the kind of person with whom others can communicate and feel at ease.
'Opt out', 'run away' when the going gets rough. Don't expect to rely on me. Self comes first. 'Look after number one' is my motto.	Blessed are those who are persecuted for righteousness' sake, for theirs is the kingdom of Heaven.	– Do what's right even when it's not popular. – Be prepared to 'stand up and be counted'. – Believe in something greater and bigger than yourselves, worth living and even worth dying for.

I am with you always

Conclusion

Thus we can see a number of elements in the Christian challenge. Firstly, we are called to resist the attractions of superficial living and false promises of happiness. Secondly, we are called to be part of the answer to the struggles of society, to be part of that new vision for the world which is presented in the Sermon on the Mount. Thirdly, we are called to recognise that humankind needs a saviour, because people are incapable of their own salvation or that of the world. This is the fundamental difference between Christianity and what is called humanism. Humanism has much in common with Christianity. The ideas put forward by Mikhail Gorbachev are very similar to the second element in the Christian concept of salvation as described in the Beatitudes. But a Christian recognises that human effort alone is not enough. Only God is truly capable of being saviour. Only God can ultimately satisfy our restlessness and fulfil our deepest longings. Only God can bring true peace and justice to the world. The idea then becomes something of a divine and human partnership – God and humanity working together to bring about the Kingdom. This perfect partnership was realised in the person of Jesus Christ in whom the two elements of salvation, the promises of God and our human response, came together. The divine promise, the covenant first made with Abraham, becomes reality in Jesus.

The Sacrifice of Abraham from Moone High Cross

God as saviour was revealed in Jesus Christ. What does this mean? How did people recognise God as saviour in Jesus Christ? Dick Westley puts it like this:

> They noticed that whenever they were in his presence they felt freer than they had ever felt before. After encountering him, they found it hard to stay centred on themselves, their cares and concerns, as their attention began to shift noticeably outwards towards others.

In the same way Jesus showed us the perfect human response to God in following him.

> To walk with the Lord is to have the very same effect on people as he did. After encountering us, do people feel freer, fear less, walk taller, sing more joyfully and feel more alive than ever before?

Redemptive Intimacy

179

The experience of indifference	a. leads to practical unbelief b. originates in our superficial experience of the world.
The challenge to awaken	a. Love and suffering are the two great awakeners. – Shirley Valentine – Alfred Prufrock
The challenge to be free	a. This is the basic Christian challenge or struggle. b. This challenge or struggle is difficult, therefore we often resist it.
The challenge of the world	– To build the Kingdom of God on earth.

Revision questions and exercises

1. 'Christianity has not been tried and found wanting, rather it has been found hard and "not tried",' (G. K. Chesterton). Discuss.

2. 'The biggest obstacle to Christian faith today is not intellectual doubt. It is, quite simply, the unchristian life-style of so many of us who think we are good Christians. (*Handing on the Faith in the Home*, Irish Bishops' Pastoral, 1980) Discuss.

CHAPTER 13

Evil and suffering and the challenge to Christian faith

This chapter declares that evil and suffering are the greatest challenges to Christian faith. They challenge Christian faith because Christian faith says that life has meaning whereas much of the evil and suffering we see and experience seems meaningless. We look at some responses to evil and suffering in literature and by individuals. Finally, it suggests that ultimately the Christian response to evil and suffering is a person – Jesus Christ – whose life, death and resurrection show that the mystery of love is greater than the mystery of evil and of suffering.

Introduction: The Experience of Suffering

There are times when the world can seem to be a very cruel place: when we find ourselves faced with prolonged suffering in ourselves or in those we love; when we see the untimely death of a young person; when our hopes, even our most noble and unselfish hopes, are frustrated. We may be driven to wonder whether these experiences of evil and suffering do not provide us with a truer picture of the world than the days we pass in comfort and in quiet happiness. After all, misery and unimaginable deprivation are a way of life for the majority of our fellow human beings (*The Inner Truth*, Donal Murray).

Questions
1. Is it true to say that 'even the most meaningful, joyful and satisfying experiences are tinged with the reality of evil and suffering'? Explain, using examples.
2. What effect do evil and suffering have on you?
3. What do you think is the difference between evil and suffering?

The human experience of evil and suffering is universal. Few can avoid such experiences – no one can avoid death.

Even the most meaningful, joyful and satisfying experiences are tinged with the reality of evil and suffering when we feel something may go wrong, these experiences will not last. The birth of a baby, for example, is usually such an occasion for joy – yet we know that this new life will inevitably end in death.

Evil and suffering are part of the history of humankind and they are realities of our own time. Indeed, in an age when so much seems possible, when scientific and technological developments have gone beyond our wildest dreams, it seems particularly unacceptable that evil and suffering continue to exist, that death remains unconquered. Moreover, it can be argued that modern progress makes the existence of suffering even more intolerable instead of lessening it. With so many advances in modern medicine, we are angry when cancer or heart disease cannot be controlled and a loved one is taken. In a developed age like ours where human fulfilment is emphasised, evil, suffering, and death seem like an attack on the successes that have been achieved by science and technology. Our modern system of mass communications makes us more aware of the suffering of others but does not provide us with a solution. President Mary Robinson drew our attention to this when she visited Somalia in October 1992 and gave her reaction to what she had seen at a press conference in Nairobi.

> I saw the images on television before I came and I found them disturbing. I found that I was moved to tears once or twice when I saw the coverage by the Irish television media. It's much more difficult when you come here, because then it's not contained in a little box – you can't go away for a cup of coffee, you can't take a telephone call. What you've got to see, as we saw for the last three days, is unacceptable.
>
> *The Irish Times*, 6 December 1992

At the end of the day, we are still left with the question, 'What is the meaning of suffering, evil, death, which have not been eliminated by all this progress?' (*Gaudium et spes*, 10)

Evil and Suffering – A challenge to Christian faith

This is a question which poses a particular challenge to the believer. Suffering is a challenge to the person who believes in God, because faith says that life has purpose and meaning. If we do not believe in God, life is either absurd, or we create our own meaning, our own happiness and only we can assume responsibility for it. There can be no indignation, no blaming of the divine if we do not experience happiness or if evil and suffering cause life to be meaningless. While we may try to alleviate evil and suffering there is no compulsion to find a meaning for such experiences.

For someone who does believe, however, the existence of evil and suffering poses a number of questions:

1. What control, what involvement, does God have in the world that he created?
2. If God made the world good, why does it contain so much evil?
3. If God is all-loving and all-powerful, why does he allow people to suffer?

 Question
How would you answer each of the above questions?

These are the questions of this chapter. They are crucial questions because the existence of evil and suffering is perhaps the greatest challenge to Christian faith. In his novel *The Brothers Karamazov*, Fyodor Dostoyevsky focuses on the problem of freedom, evil and the suffering of the innocent. Through the character of Ivan Karamazov, he presents one of the strongest arguments against God and the meaninglessness of creation – the seemingly pointless suffering of innocent children.

The story is set in Russia in the 1870s. It concerns a mean and notorious landowner, Fyodor Karamazov, and his three sons – Dimitry, an army officer, Ivan, a writer with revolutionary ideas and Alyosha, a novice in a monastery.

The family meet to solve a family dispute in the presence of a monk, Zossima. At one point, there is a lengthy conversation between Ivan and Alyosha, where Ivan uses the examples of the sufferings of innocent children to challenge Alyosha's belief in a 'dear and kind God'. He rejects the idea put forward by religion that good comes out of suffering:

Listen, if all have to suffer to buy eternal harmony by their suffering, what have the children to do with it – tell me please? It is entirely incomprehensible why they too should have to suffer and why they should have to buy harmony by their sufferings.

Then he asks who would want to be God, setting out human destiny,

...with the aim of making men happy in the end, of giving them peace and contentment at last, but that to do that it is absolutely necessary, and indeed quite inevitable, to torture to death only one tiny creature, the little girl who beat her breast with her fist.... would you consent to be the architect of those conditions?'

So powerful were Ivan's arguments that Dostoyevsky himself was afraid that he would not come up with an adequate answer:

Nowhere in Europe is so powerful a defence of atheism to be found.

In our search for an answer to the questions which evil and suffering pose for the believer, we share Dostoyevsky's fear – namely, that the awfulness, the depth and the extent of humankind's experience of evil and suffering may simply be too difficult to reconcile with belief in an all-powerful and an all-loving God. We are mindful too that easy or pat answers do not do justice or give comfort to many of our fellow human beings who are the victims of evil and suffering. Finally, as with Job in the Old Testament, we recognise our own limitations. We know that our minds are simply too small to question God or to understand his purposes.

> Where were you when I laid the foundations of the earth? Tell me if you have understanding. Who determined its measurements? – surely you know (Job 38:4,5).

For the believer then, the final answer to the meaning of evil and suffering is in the mind of God and therefore beyond complete human understanding. Yet this does not mean that we cannot make some attempt at reconciling the reality of evil and suffering with our belief in a good and just God, however limited our understanding may be.

The mystery of evil

To a great extent, the mystery of life is concerned with the conflict between good and evil. It is not surprising then that literature and drama, which so often deal with the bigger questions of life, reflect this theme. Consider any of Shakespeare's plays with which you are familiar. The dark forces of the human heart – greed, jealousy, ambition, lust and revenge – are embodied in characters like Iago, Macbeth, Claudius, Goneril and Regan.

In 'Othello', Iago is presented as the personification of evil. He delights in the pleasures of evil while appearing to be good:

> 'not I for love and duty,
> But seeming so for my peculiar end:'
> (Act I.i)

> 'Divinity of hell!
> When devils will their blackest sins
>   put on,
> They do suggest at first with
>   heavenly shows,
> As I do now.'
> (Act II.iii)

Questions and Exercise
1. Examine the theme of evil in any of Shakespeare's plays which you have studied.
2. What forms does such evil take?
3. What does Shakespeare present as the cause of evil?

In 'Macbeth' we witness the steady moral decline of the noble Macbeth – the loyal and brave general, whose tragic flaw is ambition.
Prompted by Lady Macbeth, his 'fiendlike queen', he becomes an assassin, a butcher, a monster who is hell-bound. She invokes evil itself to assist her:

'Come you spirits
That tend on mortal thoughts, unsex me here,
And fill me from the crown to the toe top-full
Of direst cruelty! Make thick my blood;
Stop up the access and passage to remorse...'
(Act I.v)

In 'Hamlet' we find the irredeemable character of Claudius, who cannot find peace or for-giveness because he is unwilling to abandon his evil ways, and the comforts he has gained from them:
'"Forgive me my foul murder"?
That cannot be, since I am still possessed
Of those effects for which I did the murder,
My crown, mine own ambition, and my queen.'
(Act III.iii)

'My words fly up, my thoughts remain below.
Words without thoughts never to heaven go.'
(Act III.iii)

In 'King Lear', the ageing King has divided his kingdom between two of his daughters, Goneril and Regan, and plans to live with each of them in turn, only to discover that he is not wanted by either. The hurt of this rejection forces him to cry out to Goneril:
'Ingratitude! thou marble-hearted fiend,
more hideous when thou show'st thee in a child
Than the sea monster.'
(Act I.iv)

Later Goneril's husband Albany describes her thus:
'See thyself, devil!
Proper deformity sees not in the fiend
So horrid as in woman.'
(Act IV.ii)

Question
What does it mean to say that 'the most radical form of evil has its source in the human heart'? Do you agree?

Evil takes many forms. We can distinguish between what we might call *cosmic evil* or natur-al disasters like hurricanes, earthquakes, floods and droughts, and *physical evil* which includes sickness, disability, deformity and death itself. However, the most radical form of evil has its source in the human heart. This *moral evil* is to be found in groups and in individuals. In individuals we identify it as ruthlessness, hatred, selfishness and bullying. In groups or in society we see it take the form of extreme nationalism (eg. Nazi Germany), or war, or economic greed where the First World grows fat while the Third World starves. In Shakespeare's plays, tragedies do not simply happen, nor are they sent. They proceed mainly from people's actions.

In our own hearts too, we find the dark forces of greed and selfishness. St Paul puts it in the form of a puzzle:

> I do not understand my own actions.
> For I do not do what I want, but I do the very
> thing I hate.... I can will what is right, but I cannot do it (Rom 7:15,18).

Exercise
Reflect on St Paul's puzzle as it applies to your life.

In his novel *Lord of the Flies,* William Golding describes the descent into barbarism of a sophisticated group of English schoolboys. Their plane crashes and they find themselves alone on a beautiful island. They gradually turn into a pack of savages and end up killing two boys, Simon and Piggy, who do not want to join their group. At the end of the novel when the boys are rescued, the island has been devastated. Only one boy has remained uncorrupted. His name is Ralph. Upon meeting his rescuers

> ... the tears began to flow and sobs shook him. He gave himself up to them now for the first time on the island, great, shuddering spasms of grief that seem to wrench his whole body. His voice rose under the black smoke before the burning wreckage of the island; and infected by that emotion, the other little boys began to shake and sob too. And in the middle of them, with filthy body, matted hair and unwiped nose, Ralph wept for the end of innocence, the darkness of man's heart, and the fall though the air of the true, wise friend called Piggy.

Human freedom and evil

What we are really saying here is that the problem of evil has its origin in the mystery of human freedom. Indeed, it is probably more correct to describe evil as a mystery rather than a problem, for it is not just a question, something that requires an answer or an explanation – it is a personal experience. It has its roots in human freedom.

> We have been free – free to choose evil courses as well as good. Free will which is our glory, distinguishing us from the animals, has also caused our sorrow.... It is not God but men who have made wars and devised ever more devastating weapons of destruction or enslavement. Why should we blame God for the concentration camps, or for the new and terrifying concept of megadeath by radiation?
>
> *Blessings,* Mary Craig

Question

1. 'Evil has its origin in the mystery of human freedom.' How true is this?

If, then, God were to be accused of anything, it would be that he has made us free. He chose to create not just stones and plants and animals but also people who have the freedom to say yes or no, even to God. Yes, God did take a risk in making us free and the evidence of this is within us and all around us, but the alternative would have been to make robots – 'creatures' who could not do wrong – but who could not love or make sacrifices or forgive either. Kill human freedom and you kill spontaneity, generosity and laughter too. Would it be worth it? Would we want to miss the joy of a restored friendship, the gratitude of the realisation that we are loved unconditionally whatever we have done and even when we least deserve it? Yes, the price of human freedom is high but we would only truly rebel, truly wish to hand back our freedom if we believed that evil has the final say, that evil wins over good. The human heart has darker forces but the drive towards the good is as strong – even stronger. This is the essence of the Christian response to evil, that God created a world in which sin abounds, but also a world in which his love, grace and mercy are even more abundant. (*Man and his Problems in the Light of Christ*, Latourelle)

Some responses to the mystery of evil

a. the response in literature

The hope, the desire that good will triumph over evil is as much part of the human heart as are the forces of evil themselves. Despite the fact that evil exists in our hearts and in our world there is much evidence that good wins out in the end – that evil does not have the final say. Consider the fairytales we were told as children – no, the wicked step-sisters did not triumph – Cinderella finally married her prince. Look at the plot in so many wild west movies – the 'baddies' have their day, but justice prevails in the end. Look at some of the Greek tragedies. We are probably most familiar with the one of the Trojan War and the wooden horse. The King of Troy had abducted Helen, the wife of the King of Sparta. This led to a war between the Trojans and the Greeks which lasted for ten years. Finally, the Greeks, appearing defeated, sent a 'gift' of a wooden horse to the Trojans who took it within the walls of their city. The Greek soldiers who had been hidden inside opened the gates of the city and let their army in. Finally, having defeated the Trojans, the Greeks returned home in triumph, bringing Helen with them. Order had been restored. Justice had been done.

Earlier, we considered evil in some of Shakespeare's plays. We know them as 'tragedies'. This idea of tragedy implies that evil is not the natural human state. People have flaws. People do evil, people descend into evil and this brings chaos. This is the tragedy. Evil is a distortion of the natural state of people and of the world. In the end there is the attempt to restore order and the natural state of things.

In 'Othello,' Lodovico says to Cassio about Iago:
> 'To you, Lord governor,
> Remains the censure of this hellish villain
> The time, the place, the torture: O, enforce it! (Act V.ii)

Othello recognises the folly of his own deeds:
> 'Of one whose hand
> like the base Judean, threw a pearl away,
> Richer than all his tribe.' (Act V.ii)

In 'Macbeth' both Macbeth and Lady Macbeth suffer the consequences of indulging in evil. She is driven insane.
> 'Unnatural deeds
> Do breed unnatural troubles; infected minds
> To their deaf pillows will discharge their secrets.
> More needs she the divine than a physician.' (Act V.i)

Macbeth learns the harsh reality of trusting in evil:
> 'I pull in resolution, and begin
> To doubt the equivocation of the fiend,
> That lies like truth.' (Act V.v)

Hamlet's problem has been procrastination – this allows the evil of others to thrive while justice waits to be done. At the finale, the subterfuge and evil plots are exposed. Justice is done and the natural order is restored.

> 'And let me speak to th' yet unknowing world
> How these things came about. So shall you hear
> Of carnal, bloody, and unnatural acts....
> And, in this upshot, purposes mistook
> Fall'n on the inventors' heads.' (Horatio, Act V.ii)

> 'The foul practice
> Hath turned itself on me.'   (Laertes, Act V.ii)

In 'King Lear', the perpetrators of evil eventually meet their downfall. Cornwall, the heartless husband of Regan, dies as a result of his evil actions. Whilst torturing Gloucester, Cornwall is so brutal as to provoke even a servant into defending the old man – and is thus mortally wounded. The news of his death is greeted by the noble Albany:

> 'This shows you are above,
> You justicers, that these our nether crimes
> So speedily can venge.'   (Act IV.ii)

Albany later assumes command of the kingdom and restores order:

> 'All friends shall taste
> The wages of their virtue, and all foes
> The cup of their deservings.'   (Act V.iii)

b. the response of people

Moving away from literature and looking to more concrete examples of the triumph of good over evil, consider the story of Anne Frank, the young Dutch Jewish girl who spent most of the years of the Second World War in a secret hideout in Amsterdam. During this time, she kept a diary. We might expect it to reveal hatred and bitterness towards the Nazis, yet, on 15 July 1944 she wrote:

> This is the difficulty in these times: ideals, dreams and cherished hopes rise within us, only to meet the horrible truth and be shattered. It's really a wonder that I haven't dropped all my ideals, because they seem so absurd and impossible to carry out. Yet I keep them in spite of everything. I still believe that people are good at heart. I simply cannot build up my hopes on a foundation consisting of confusion, misery and death.

On 8 November 1987, Remembrance Day, Gordon Wilson's daughter Marie was killed along with others by an IRA bomb in Enniskillen. Many people expected reprisal, revenge for this barbaric act. Then came the words of Gordon Wilson, spoken through heartbroken grief:

> I bear no ill-will. I bear no grudge. That sort of talk is not going to bring her back to life. She was a great wee lassie. She loved her profession. She was a pet. She's dead. She's in heaven. Don't ask me, please, for a purpose. I don't have a purpose. I don't have an answer. But I know there has to be a plan.... It's part of a greater plan. And God is good. And we shall meet again.

How can the human spirit survive such evil? How can the human spirit forgive and not be consumed by anger? How could Gordon Wilson utter the words that he did? This is perhaps as great a mystery as that of evil itself.

Question
What answers would you give to these questions?

c. the Christian response

We saw part of the answer to these questions in chapter 3 in the words of Victor Frankl, himself a survivor of concentration camps. The salvation of man is through love and in love. This is the essence of the Christian response to evil – the mystery of God's love revealed in Jesus Christ is greater than the mystery of evil. The Christian message does not give us an explanation for the existence of evil. Rather as in Dostoyevsky's story, the response to evil is a person – an action and not an argument. Dostoyevsky's answer was the monk Zossimus – his life, his person, his example, his love.

Oscar Wilde

In 'De Profundis,' Oscar Wilde also saw the connection between suffering and love:

'I used to say that there was enough suffering in one narrow London lane to show that God did not love man, and that wherever there was any sorrow, though but that of a little child in some garden weeping over a fault he had not committed, the whole face of creation was completely marred. I was entirely wrong. I was not in the sphere in which belief was to be attained to. Now it seems to me that love of some kind is the only possible explanation of the extraordinary amount of suffering there is in the world. I cannot conceive of any other explanation.'

So too, God's answer is not an explanation, it is a person, his son, who himself dies on the cross. The crucified Christ brings into the world a love that is greater than all the hatred there may ever be. Love wins over evil not by force but by sheer excess.

We can see what is meant by this if we examine the experience of love and hatred in our own lives. If we do wrong or if we have wrong done to us, the natural reaction is often to meet wrong with wrong. Yet think about how disarmed we feel when our wrong is met not by revenge or by defence but by overwhelming love. Our temper fades, we are silenced. Love has overcome hate. If there is, then, any victory over evil it is to be won by a love that rises above hate.

In this sense then, Christianity does not get rid of evil, sin and death. As one theologian put it: 'It is not a religion of consolation or of escape but a religion of conversion' – a conversion that is possible because of the extravagant love of God.

> But when he came to himself he said, 'How many of my father's hired servants have bread enough to spare, but I perish here with hunger. I will arise and go to my father and I will say to him, "Father I have sinned against heaven and before you; I am no longer worthy to be called your son; treat me as one of your hired servants."'
> And he arose and came to his father. But while he was yet at a distance, his father saw him and had compassion, and ran and embraced him and kissed him. (Lk 15:17-20)

Yes, 'God sent his son into the world not to condemn the world, but that the world might be saved through him' (Jn 3:16-17). This is the Christian response to the mystery of evil. When evil seems to us more violent, more ugly, more cruel than anything we could have imagined, then we know that we are not big enough to face evil alone. Then we know that we need to be saved through Jesus.

Question
1. How valid a response to evil is it to say that 'if there is any victory over evil, it is to be won by a love that rises above hate'?

The mystery of suffering

> My God, my God, why have you abandoned me?
> I have cried desperately for help,
> but still it does not come.
> During the day I call to you, my God,
> but you do not answer;
> I call at night,
> but get no rest.
>
> Ps 22:1,2

a. Suffering as teacher

The psalmist in the Old Testament utters the same cry against God as do many who suffer. Why does God allow suffering to exist? We can accept that there are certain forms of suffering that make us better people. We often hear people speak of the 'school of suffering'. When we look back on our own lives we can think of many experiences, which we would not have chosen, which seemed very painful at the time but in which we now see value. Leaving home, sacrificing our free time for study or training may only seem worthwhile when we see the end product. The things we might consider disasters in our lives – an exam we failed, a match we lost, a relationship that ended, may well prove in time not to be so disastrous at all. On seeing a broader picture of our lives we may realise how we have grown through such experiences. Think of the admiration we hold, the sense of reverence we feel before someone who has become wise and mature through suffering.

? Question

In your experience can suffering serve as a teacher? How?

Sometimes great things are born only of suffering. Sometimes too the experience of suffering can make us sensitive to other people.

> I have lost my parents – I know what sadness is.
> I have been in prison – I know what loneliness is.
> I have lived with the destitute and I know what want is.
> I have sat with the dying, and I know what fear is.
>
> Simon Community Worker, Limerick

To be able to love, to open out towards other people is at the same time to be able to suffer, to be vulnerable with other people. To know no sorrow, may also be to know no love.

The poet Richard Shannon puts it like this:

> How exquisite and how perfect is the living flower which knows both birth and death: while the plastic flower which lasts a thousand years is ever brutal in its changelessness. The softness of one and the hardness of the other. It is vulnerability that makes one open and beautiful. And surely without death (without suffering), there is no vulnerability. *The Peacock and the Phoenix*

A world in which suffering occurs is the only kind of world where courage, loyalty and compassion as we know them could exist. The following prayer was found written on a piece of wrapping paper near the body of a dead child in Ravensbruck concentration camp where 92,000 women and children died.

> O Lord,
> remember not only the men and women of good will,
> but also those of ill will.
> But do not only remember the suffering they have inflicted on us.
> Remember the fruits which brought thanks to this suffering.
> Our comradeship, our loyalty, our humility, the courage, the generosity, the greatness of heart which has grown out of all of this.
> And when they come to judgment let all the fruits that we have borne be their forgiveness.

b. Suffering as a challenge to Christian faith

Yet, despite all of these considerations, there is too much suffering in our world and in our history. Moreover, suffering does not always lead to growth. What growth takes place in the dying baby who has starved to death? Why does God not do something about pointless suffering? The first thing that has to be said here is that God did not intend people to suffer. Much of the suffering in the world is caused by people. If God were to intervene to end such suffering then people would no longer be free. But this does not answer the suffering which is caused not by people but by illness and natural disasters. This is the real question of suffering which challenges faith. *Ultimately no one has answered this question sufficiently. Christ himself did not offer an explanation for suffering. Instead he accepted, shared and changed it.* Thus, instead of suffering being a reason for despair, it becomes an opportunity, a moment for salvation. Suffering thus acquires a meaning – its purpose is salvation. How can this happen? While we are smug and self-sufficient we feel no need of a saviour – we create our own happiness. Suffering can break through the hardness of our selfishness and our pride and open us up to God and to our fellow human beings. Oscar Wilde describes this possibility in his poem 'The Ballad of Reading Gaol'.

> Ah! happy they whose hearts can break
> And peace of pardon win!
> How else may man make straight his plan
> and cleanse his soul from sin?
> How else but through a broken heart
> May Lord Christ enter in?

The cross of Jesus Christ is the ultimate answer to the meaning of suffering. The person of Jesus, rather than an explanation, is God's response to the mystery of suffering. We cannot fully understand the why of suffering but we need not despair. Christian faith says that ultimately God is there with us even in the darkest moments.

> Think of the flowers growing in the fields;
> they never have to work or spin; yet I assure you not even Solomon in all his glory was like one of these. Now if that is how God clothes the grass in the field which is here today and thrown into the furnace tomorrow, will he not much more look after you, you men of little faith? (Mt 6:25-30)

Footprints

One night a man had a dream. He dreamed he was walking along the beach with the Lord. Across the sky flashed scenes from his life. For each scene, he noticed two sets of footprints in the sand; one belonging to him, and the other to the Lord.

When the last scene of his life flashed before him, he looked back at the footprints in the sand. He noticed that many times along the path of his life there was only one set of footprints. He also noticed that it happened at the very lowest and saddest times in his life.

This really bothered him and he questioned the Lord about it. 'Lord, you said that once I decided to follow you, you'd walk with me all the way. But I have noticed that during the most troublesome times in my life, there is only one set of footprints. I don't understand why when I needed you most you would leave me.'

The Lord replied, 'My precious, precious child, I love you and I would never leave you. During your times of trial and suffering, when you saw only one set of footprints, it was then that I carried you.'

The cross of Jesus assures us that God knows suffering – not as an observer or simply as an outsider, but rather as a participant, in other words from inside out. As a result,

> the cross helps us to live in hope with suffering and to realise at the same time that we do not suffer alone or in vain.

Christ at the Centre, Dermot Lane

So our reaction as Christians to the mystery of suffering is twofold. In faith and with confidence, we surrender to the will of God, believing that somehow all will be well. Secondly, we participate with Christ in the struggle against illness, hunger and suffering, knowing that the final solution will not be had on earth, but rather in the new earth and the new heaven, where there will be no more crying or mourning or pain (Rv 21).

SUMMARY CHART

1. The mystery of evil	a. a human experience
	b. moral evil has its source in the human heart – and its origin in the mystery of human freedom
	c. responses to the mystery of evil
	  – in literature
	  – in people
	  – the Christian response

2. The mystery of suffering	a. suffering as teacher b. suffering as a challenge to Christian faith c. The person of Jesus, rather than any explanation as a response to the mystery of suffering

Revision questions and exercises

1. 'Evil and suffering are the greatest challenge to Christian faith'. Discuss.
2. How useful did you find the assertion that love, and ultimately the love of Jesus, rather than an explanation, is the Christian response to the mystery of suffering?
3. What response would you give to the mystery of evil and suffering?

CHAPTER 14

'If Christ had not been raised from the dead your faith is in vain'

1 Cor 15:14

This chapter considers the ultimate challenge to Christian faith, namely death. 'If Christ had not been raised from the dead, your faith is in vain.' It acknowledges that death is part of life, that life is transient. Yet the seeds of immortality are also to be found in human experience. The seeds of resurrection, the seeds of eternal life, find their first home in the heart of the human person. Christianity does not deny death – it gives it new meaning, in the life, death and resurrection of Jesus.

These are only hints and guesses.
Hints followed by guesses; and the rest
is prayer, observance, discipline, thought and action.
The hint half guessed, the gift half understood, is Incarnation.

T.S. Eliot, The Dry Salvages, *Four Quartets*

Introduction: The reality of death

In the previous chapter, we acknowledged that the human experience of evil and suffering is universal. Few can avoid such experiences – no one can avoid death. Most of us fear death, whether it be our own death or that of someone we love.

Our modern world tends to mask the reality of death. In the Middle Ages and, indeed, right into this century, epidemics, war and lack of medical expertise all made life short and brought death nearer to people. We know for instance that the Black Plague of 1348 claimed 25 million lives. The Second World War cost 26 million lives. In Ireland up to 1949, tuberculosis claimed between 3,000 and 4,000 lives a year. Today, advances in medicine, better food and less physical hardship have helped to ensure that many people live their 'three score and ten years'. Such changes have resulted in different attitudes towards death. In the past when death came earlier to people than it does today, there was a more open acceptance of death. The sick person was told that death was imminent. When the person did die, it was usually at home and in the presence of the family. The wake held in the house ensured that people, even young people, were brought close to the reality of death.

Today, death has become a taboo subject. Sometimes it can seem that we do everything we can to avoid encountering this end that we fear. Think of the great efforts made not to let people know that they are dying. Everyone conspires to hide this fact from the dying person – 'You're looking much better today.' 'It won't be long before you're up and about again.' The irony is that the dying person is often aware of the truth but does not discuss it for fear of upsetting those who are close. This means that he or she is isolated in the fears, anxieties and thoughts about what he or she is about to face. How uncomfortable would it make us feel if the dying person expressed a wish to discuss impending death? Perhaps this is because it reminds us of our own mortality. We do everything to avoid thinking and talking about death. Even the very language we use illustrates this. We speak about someone 'departing', 'passing away', 'gone'.

Nowadays people often die in hospital, removed from their homes and their families. Even when they do die at home, the body is often whisked away to a funeral home where an elaborate setting tends to camouflage the reality of the person's death. The weeping, crying and wailing associated with mourning at funerals in previous times does not seem acceptable any more. People try to avoid scenes of broken-hearted grief. We hear comments like, 'He held up well,' and 'She was very composed.' We tend to admire those who can be 'strong', while we feel uncomfortable and embarrassed if someone 'breaks down'.

Questions
1. Why do we fear death so much?
2. Is the subject of death a real issue for young people?

The fear of death

Why do we fear death so much? One answer to this question is that death is *the* great unknown, the great uncertainty in our lives. No matter how rough this life may be we know to some extent what we are facing. Others who have faced similar experiences are there to tell us – not so with death. We cannot 'try out' death. No one has come back to tell us what it is like. In the opening scene of Shakespeare's 'Hamlet' – we find Hamlet, the so-called great philosopher prince of the Middle Ages in a very thoughtful, very melancholic mood. His father has died. His mother is involved in an improper relationship (an affair with her brother-in-law). His father's ghost has set Hamlet a task – to avenge the death of his father. Hamlet is deeply troubled by the prospect of this task. In this scene he agonises over whether he should continue to suffer the trials of life or whether he should commit suicide.

> 'To be or not to be: that is the question:
> Whether 'tis nobler in the mind to suffer
> The slings and arrows of outrageous fortune,
> Or take up arms against a sea of troubles
> And by opposing end them.' (III.i)

Then Hamlet considers what will happen if he does take his own life. Will he have peace? Death has been compared to sleep, but he has suffered nightmares in his own sleep. Therefore will death not cause him similar suffering? This is the great unknown, the source of his fear.

> 'To die, to sleep –
> to sleep – perchance to dream: ay,
> There's the rub.
> For in that sleep of death, what dreams may come
> When we have shuffled off this mortal coil,
> Must give us pause.' (III.i).

Question
Explain Hamlet's dilemma as presented in Act III.i.

The transience of life

No matter how little we know about death, no matter how much we fear death or try to mask that fear, death is the one sure thing in our lives. When we cannot sleep, because someone we know and love is suffering and is going to die, death is no longer an abstract idea for us. It becomes something that concerns us personally. Perhaps it is only at moments like these that we begin to realise that in a sense all of life is tinged with death. Nothing in the natural world, no one we know, no experience we have, lasts forever. Everything is transient, everything passes away. So many poets from Shakespeare to Keats have contemplated this truth.

'When I consider everything that grows
Holds in perfection but a little moment...
When I perceive that men as plants increase,
Cheered and check'd e'en by the self-same sky,
Vaunt in their youthful sap, at height decrease
And wear their brave state out of memory.'

Sonnet No. 15, Shakespeare

Exercise
Imagine that you are writing a sonnet on the transience of life.
What lines would you substitute for Shakespeare's?

Keats is more personal in his realisation that life does not last, that death is inevitable, that he will not live forever.

When I have fears that I may cease to be
Before my pen has glean'd my teeming brain,
When I behold, upon the night's starr'd face
Huge cloudy symbols of a high romance,
And think that I may never live to trace
Their shadows, with the magic hand of chance.

'Terror of Death'

Exercise
Compare Shakespeare's reflections on the transience of life with those
of Keats.

Some responses to the reality of death

Given that death is such a universal and certain reality it is no wonder that it has occupied the minds of some of the greatest thinkers throughout the ages.

1. Plato

Four hundred years before Christ, the Greek philosopher Plato thought of death as that experience which separates the body from the soul. The body dies, the immortal soul lives on. Plato considered the body to be a prison for the soul from which the soul wanted to be released to an eternal and true life with knowledge and contemplation about eternal truths like justice, love and the good. (We have already considered some of Plato's ideas on these virtues in chapter 3.) Thus for Plato the moment of death is the great moment for, from now on, the mortal part of the person – the body – is no more, while the immortal soul, untouched by death, lives on.

2. Jean-Paul Sartre

For the French atheistic philosopher, Jean Paul Sartre, life itself has whatever meaning we can give it. Life is a project, we make what we can of it – therefore death has no meaning at all. Indeed death robs life of any meaning. There is no motive for our being born – there is no meaning in our death. We can invest any meaning we can in the gap which lies between but that is all.

3. Albert Camus

For Albert Camus, another atheistic philosopher, life itself is absurd and meaningless. It is full of suffering and ends in death. Life tries to be meaningful but it only has the first word – death always has the last. What can we do? We must first accept that life is absurd and then we must try to give meaning to this absurdity. How do we do this? By sharing in the suffering and death of others. This is the only meaning we can create for our lives – the value of solidarity with the suffering world.

4. Marx

In Marxist philosophy the individual has value only in relation to society. The value of someone's life is in their contribution to the progress of society – the advancement of the cause. Thus, when the individual dies, it is not a source of personal loss and suffering. The Party, the new world, will continue to be built. One dies knowing that one has contributed to the advancement of humankind – the work will go on. If there is a heaven it is in the hearts of those who are left – those fellow workers who will continue the struggle, inspired by the one who has departed this life.

Question and exercise
1. Compare the responses of these four philosophers to the reality of death.
2. Which response, if any, is nearest your own response to the fact of death?

The human desire for immortality

For many, as we have seen, death is the end. What meaning there is exists in our lives here and now. Yet from the beginning of time, human beings have sought to overcome death and achieve immortality. The elaborate burial customs of ancient peoples, from New Grange to the Pyramids of Egypt, all bear witness to the fact that people have not been content to accept death as their final end. Myths like the Irish story of Tír na nÓg – the land where no one will grow old – are part of the folklore of every nation. Consider the fascination people have with stories of people who 'died' for a few minutes, saw a light at the end of a dark tunnel and then came back to life again.

Consider too all the ways in which people try to achieve immortality. For some it is through their children. For others it is through the mark they leave on society or on history. For poets like Yeats and Keats the only immortality is through art.

> Once out of nature I shall never take
> My bodily form from any natural thing,
> But such a form as Grecian goldsmiths make
> Of hammered gold and gold enamelling.
>
> 'Sailing to Byzantium', W.B. Yeats

Few of us are content to feel that our life will simply be snuffed out. We like to feel that at least we have left some mark on this earth, that we will not be gone and forgotten almost as if we never lived. It may be difficult to believe in some form of after-life but to accept that death is really the end is equally difficult. In his story, 'Ward No. 6', Anton Chekhov presents two characters, a doctor and a postmaster, who suddenly find themselves discussing the human soul.

'And you do not believe in the immortality of the soul?' the postmaster asks suddenly. 'No, honoured Mikhail Averyanitch; I do not believe it, and have no grounds for believing it.' 'I must own I doubt it too,' Mikhaivl Averyanitch admits. 'And yet I have a feeling as though I should never die. Oh, I think to myself: 'Old fogey, it is time you were dead!' But there is a little voice in my soul that says: 'Don't believe it; you won't die.'

In so many ways, we rebel against death. Vatican II gives this explanation for our rebellion:

Because he bears in himself the seeds of eternity, which cannot be reduced to mere matter, he rebels against death.

Gaudium et spes, 18

 Question
Why do you think people find it so difficult to accept death as the end?

To say that people have within themselves the seeds of eternity is to say that just as all of life is tinged with death, so too all of life is tinged with resurrection. If we look both at the natural world and at human experience we can see what is meant by this. Everything that dies, everything that ends gives rise to something else. Winter dies so that spring is born. Childhood comes to an end so that adulthood may begin. The seed dies so that the plant may live. The writer C.S.Lewis goes a step further than this. He argues that our very restlessness as human beings, our sense of dissatisfaction with this world is itself an indication that death and this world are not our final end.

If you really are a product of a materialistic universe, how is it you don't feel at home there? Do fish complain at the sea for being wet? Or if they did, would that fact itself not strongly suggest that they had not always been or would not always be aquatic creatures?

Perhaps it is this very experience of not feeling quite at home in the world that has pointed people towards belief in an afterlife. It is the same idea that we found in St Augustine where the restlessness of the human heart points towards God. So too the very desire for immortality that also rests in the human heart could be said to point towards some form of eternity, some form of heaven. Thus, as we consider the resurrection of Jesus Christ and the Christian response to death, we can say that it is not totally outside human experience. The seeds of resurrection, the seeds of eternal life, find their first home in the heart of the human person, in the desire to overcome death, in the desire for immortality.

The Christian response to death

The title of this chapter is taken from St Paul's letter to the Corinthians:

> If Christ had not been raised from the dead, your faith is in vain.
>
> (1 Cor 15:14)

In other words, the foundation of the hope which we talked about in chapter 1 and the victory over evil and suffering which we discussed in chapter 3 mean nothing if death still wins out in the end. Indeed, if Christ had not risen from the dead, we would not even be considering a Christian response to death. Jesus Christ, the founder of Christianity, would simply have gone down in history as one who had lived a good and kindly life. At the time, even his disciples saw his death as the end of their hopes. They returned to their families disappointed and resigned. His death made them feel that the one who had promised so much, who had raised so many hopes, had been defeated.

Questions
1. Could Jesus have avoided his death?
2. Had he made that choice, what would it have said about his life and message?

The death of Jesus

As a human being, Jesus experienced all the helplessness, all the agony and all the aloneness which accompany death. He was spared nothing of the suffering that death brings to human beings. If anything, he suffered more than most. Crucifixion was a particularly brutal form of death.

What characterises the death of Jesus is his total surrender to the will of his Father. 'Not my will, but thine be done.' Jesus could only have avoided his death by abandoning his message. He had promised a new way of life. He had called on people to repent and to embrace this new way of life. He had, as we see in the Beatitudes, turned human priorities upside down. Moreover, he had spoken with a sense of authority which annoyed the religious leaders of the time. He suggested a special relationship between himself and his Father. In the Gospels, God is called 'Father' no less than one hundred and seventy times. Jesus did not just call God 'Father', but addressed him as 'Abba', Father, a term which implies a closeness, an intimacy with God. It is a term which was used only by a person addressing his or her own father – a bit like 'Dad' or 'Daddy'.

There were many who could not accept the radical call of Jesus to change their lives. There were many more who interpreted his understanding of his relationship with his Father as blasphemy. Faced with such opposition, Jesus had a choice: he could either abandon or renege on his message, or he could accept the consequences of remaining faithful to all he had said and done. Jesus chose the latter. If his life had revealed the love of God for humankind, his death revealed that God's love is steadfast and unconditional even in the face of death. 'No greater love than this can a man have, that he lay down his life for his friends.' Thus,

> the death of Jesus reveals to us how absolute God's love is. God's love is condition-less, expressing itself even to the point of ultimate donation in death. We are saved, not by the physical death of Jesus, but by the absoluteness of a love which did not count death too high a price.

Who is Christ? Anthony Padovano

The Resurrection of Jesus

The death of Jesus was an act of unselfish love. Yet we know that other people have accepted death for the most loving of reasons. During the Second World War the Polish priest Maximilian Kolbe willingly gave his life to save that of a fellow prisoner. What makes Jesus' death so fundamentally different from any other death, was that he rose again.

> Jesus died and rose again. The first two words are ordinary and the last two are the most startling statements ever made.

I am with you always, Bríd Greville & Brendan Halpin

The reality of the Resurrection is the cornerstone of Christian faith, yet nobody witnessed the Resurrection itself. So was the idea of a Risen Lord something which the disciples invented in order to dramatise themselves and make their message convincing? If we go along with this line of thinking, we are left with a number of problems:

1. Jesus had not died a hero's death. His disciples had no wish to be associated with him at the time of his death or immediately afterwards. Indeed, they were running away in case they met with the same fate. Peter denied him three times.

2. Initially, after Jesus' death, the disciples returned home. Later they began to meet, churches were formed and they undertook worldwide missions. What made them change their minds? Why was there such a revival of their faith after their initial sense of disappointment? It is difficult to understand how a small group of disciples, whose faith had been shattered by the scandal of the cross, could suddenly recover confidence and go forth with a renewed faith if something as dramatic as the Resurrection had not taken place.

3. Why was there no attempt to deny the empty tomb? Some soldiers were bribed to say that the body was stolen, but no attempt was made to deny that the tomb was empty.

(Mt 28:6; Mk 16:6)

4. The disciples began preaching to people, many of whom were unsympathetic to their message or to the person of Jesus. Such people would not have been slow to expose any possible fraud in the account of the Resurrection.

Exercises
1. Look up the following accounts of the Resurrection of Jesus:
   Mt 28; Mk 16:19-20; Lk 24: 13ff; Jn 20:19-30
2. Read each story, pick out the words and phrases that show that:
   a. Jesus is the same person that his followers knew.
   b. Jesus is different.

The appearances

When talking about the Resurrection, the four Gospels focus primarily on the appearances of the Risen Lord to some of his friends and followers.

On reading the accounts of the appearances, a pattern emerges:

1. Jesus' followers are dejected and disappointed.
2. The initiative for the appearance came from Jesus.
3. There was a lack of recognition on the part of those who saw Jesus.
4. Jesus gave some form of greeting, e.g. 'Do not be afraid'; 'Peace be with you.'
5. The climax of the story was the moment of recognition.
6. The story concludes with the words of command, 'Go make disciples everywhere.'

I am with you always

But Mary stood weeping outside the tomb and as she wept, she stooped to look into the tomb; and she saw two angels in white, sitting where the body of Jesus had lain, one at the head and one at the feet. They said to her, 'Woman, why are you weeping?' She said to them, 'Because they have taken away my Lord, and I do not know where they have laid him.' Saying this, she turned round and saw Jesus standing, but she did not know that it was Jesus. Jesus said to her, 'Woman, why are you weeping? Whom do you seek?' Supposing him to be the gardener, she said to him, 'Sir, if you have carried him away, tell me where you have laid him, and I will take him away.' Jesus said to her, 'Mary'. She turned and said to him in Hebrew, 'Rabboni!' (which means teacher). Jesus said to her, 'Do not hold me, for I have not yet ascended to the Father; but go to my brethren and say to them, I am ascending to my Father and your Father, to my God and your God.'

(Jn 20:11-17)

The meaning of the Resurrection

In the Preface of the Mass for the Dead, Jesus is presented as the source of our hope:

In him who rose from the dead,
our hope of resurrection dawned.
The sadness of death gives way
to the bright promise of immortality.
Lord, for your faithful people, life is changed, not ended.
When the body of our earthly dwelling lies in death,
we gain an everlasting dwelling-place in heaven.
(Preface of Christian Death I)

The concept of *transformation* or *change* is a key concept in our understanding of the Resurrection. There was something the same and yet something very different about the resurrected Jesus. This is evident in the fact that the disciples were slow to recognise him. He has changed or was transformed in some way.

> We sense in the risen Jesus a freedom that was no longer limited by time and space. He is free to be present when and where and to whom he wishes. His presence brings a joyfulness and a peace 'that surpasses all understanding'. His followers had a real experience of Jesus as being alive and present in a new way after his death. It was not easy to put such an experience into words or to express their new understanding of the mystery of the Resurrection of Jesus.

I am with you always

St Paul compares this transformation to that which happens to the seed. The seed falls on the ground, dies and gives rise to a changed or transformed stalk of wheat. Something dies so that something better may rise:

> So it is with the resurrection of the dead. What is sown is perishable, what is raised is imperishable. It is sown in dishonour, it is raised in glory. It is sown in weakness, it is raised in power. It is sown a physical body, it is raised a spiritual body.
> (1 Cor 15:42-44)

In this sense then, there is a basic unity between death and resurrection. Dermot Lane puts it like this in *Christ at the Centre:*

> There is no resurrection without death, and the death of the individual without resurrection would be the final absurdity of life. We all wish to bask in the glory of the resurrection but we shirk the way to resurrection which is the way of the cross. There can be no glory without the cross, so the law of life for the Christian becomes the law of the cross.

Thus the kind of hope offered to the Christian by the death and Resurrection of Jesus is not a kind of Utopia, somewhat removed from this world. Rather it 'sets a Christian on the way of the cross which is none other than the way of actual bodily obedience in everyday life' (*Jesus the Christ*, Walter Kasper). In this sense belief in the Resurrection is not simply a desire for immortality, some cosy assurance that death is not the end. Rather, to hope for eternal life as a Christian is to become an active sign of that hope in this life:

> This means, in effect, that as we go through life we must summon up the courage to risk dying daily in order to find ourselves, to let go of the ego to find the self in its human and divine relationship. If we fail to do this during life it is unlikely that we will know how to surrender ourselves at death into the gracious presence of the triune God (*Christ at the Centre*, Dermot A. Lane).

SUMMARY CHART

1. The reality of death
   The fear of death
   The transience of life

2. Some responses to the reality
   of death

   a. Plato: the soul lives on;
   b. Sartre: death has no meaning; we give life
      any meaning we can;
   c. Camus: life is absurd; accept this share in
      the suffering of others;
   d. Marx: only the individual dies; the new
      world will continue to be built.

3. The human desire for
   immortality

   1. Evidence
   a. burial customs
   b. myths
   c. immortality through art, through fame,
      through one's children
   2. Reasons
   a. all of life is tinged with the seeds of
      eternity/resurrection
   b. human restlessness

4. The Christian response
   to death

   a. The death of Jesus.
      – its reason/its meaning
   b. The Resurrection of Jesus
      – an invention – problems
      – the appearances
      – the meaning of the Resurrection
   i. transformation
   ii. the link between death and resurrection

Revision exercises and questions
1. Write an essay entitled 'Death is the ultimate taboo subject'.
2. The Resurrection is ultimately a matter of faith. Discuss.
3. Dying and rising are part of the everyday life of a Christian. What is
   meant by this?
4. The Resurrection of Jesus does not force faith, it presumes faith.
   Discuss.